# Vehicle Extraction Course

## Police Bujitsu Club, LLC

**FOR LAW ENFORCEMENT AGENCIES Everywhere**

Written By
**GARY G. ALBRECHT**

The author has made every effort to ensure the accuracy of the information contained in this book. The author and publisher of this book disclaim any liability, including liability for negligence, for any personal injury, property damage, or any other loss, damage, cost, claim, or expense including claims for consequential damages that the reader or others may suffer from following any of the methods of instruction provided in this book. The reader of this book recognizes and accepts this disclaimer of Liability by the author and publisher and the reader assumes the risks of using the techniques displayed in this book.

# Vehicle Extraction Course

## Police Bujitsu Club, LLC

**FOR LAW ENFORCEMENT AGENCIES Everywhere**

Written By
**GARY G. ALBRECHT**

Vehicle Extraction Course
All Rights Reserved
Copyright © 2015 Gary G. Albrecht
v2.0

**PUBLISHER'S NOTE**

The opinions expressed in this manuscript are solely the opinions of the author in addition, do not represent the opinions or thoughts of the Publisher. The author has represented and warranted full ownership and/or legal right to publish all the materials in this book.

The publisher does not have any control over and does not assume any responsibility for author or third party websites or their content.

This book may not be reproduced, transmitted, or stored in whole or in part by any means, including graphic, electronic, or mechanical without the express written consent of the publisher except in the case of brief quotations embodied in critical articles and reviews. Any reproductions without written permission from the publisher is illegal and punishable by law. Please purchase only from authorized distributors to protect the author's rights.

Harrison House Publishing
www.theharrisonhousepublishing.com
info@theharrisonhousepublising.com
ISBN: 978-0-9861071-0-8
Library of Congress Control Number: 2015952720
Harrison House Publishing and the "HH" logo are trademarks belonging to Harrison House Publishing.
PRINTED IN THE UNITED STATES OF AMERICA

# INDEX

**Acknowledgments** .................................................................... **1—2**

**Foreword** ................................................................................ **3—6**

**Introduction** ........................................................................... **7—8**

CHAPTER 1 ................................................... 9

EXTRACTION I, ELBOW HYPEREXTENSION

**Inner Voice** ............................................................................. **10 –12**

**Hand Positioning** ................................................................... **13—14**

**Vehicle Approach** .................................................................. **15**

**Elbow Hyperextension** .......................................................... **16 - 27**

**Takedown After Handcuffing** ............................................... **27- 29**

CHAPTER II ................................................. 30

EXTRACTION II, FIGURE FOUR LAPEL GRAB

**Figure Four Lapel Grab** ......................................................... **31—42**

**Control Takedown Then Handcuff** ....................................... **42 - 47**

**Standing Your Handcuffed Prisoner Technique 1** ................ **48—49**

CHAPTER III ................................................ 50

EXTRACTION III, LAPEL ELBOW HYPEREXTENSION

**Lapel Elbow Hyperextension** ................................................ **51- 58**

**Moving A Handcuffed Prisoner** ............................................. **58—60**

CHAPTER IV ................................................. 61

EXTRACTION IV, BATON HYPEREXTENSION

**Baton Hyperextension** .......................................................... **62—68**

## CHAPTER IV ................................................ 61
### EXTRACTION IV, BATON HYPEREXTENSION

**Baton Hyperextension** ................................................................ **62—68**

**Standing Handcuffed Prisoner Technique 2** ................................. **69—70**

## CHAPTER V ............................. 71
### EXTRACTION V, BENT ARM L-WRIST

**Bent Arm L-Wrist** ........................................................... **72—77**

**Bent Arm L-Wrist Takedown** ........................................... **78—84**

## Closing...................... 85

# ACKNOWLEDGMENTS

It was a great pleasure doing this book and the presentation to go with it. Without the help of the following persons, this book would have been a real chore. I can not express enough, the appreciation I have for the people that have helped me write this book.

## ANDRIES CANE

It is hard to start at a point where my thanks could even scratch the surface for all Andy has done for me. Not only the help and guidance he has given to me on this book, but the many years as my sensei and a close personal friend. The help with this book comes first with his encouragement that he gave me to write it. He did a wonderful job as the photographer for this book. His help in the editing was an ongoing job and greatly appreciated. Thank you Andy for all the help through the past 25 plus years. You have always given me direction in my life as well as in the martial arts world. Thanks……..

## Officer Jose Andrade

I would like to give a special thanks to Jose for assisting me as the suspect in the vehicle extractions that I performed all these techniques on. He was a good "Uke". He has assisted me now in two books and has done a great job. He is always willing to assist when he can. Thanks Jose, you have done a great job, and I am looking forward to years of martial arts with you as a student as well as an instructor.

## Joseph Rodriguez

With my lack of computer skills, it has kept Joseph very busy. Joseph has helped so much, day and night, not only on the book, but on the power point presentation for this course. Without his help, I don't know where I would be. My special thanks to a great friend, and a real pal.

## Detective Steve Huron

I want to say thanks for the years of friendship, and the years we worked the streets of San Antonio together. Steve also was a good student of mine in the Police Bujitsu Club. His help was not directly on the book but on the presentation portion where he is the officer taking the driver out of the car. Thanks Steve you are a real pal and brother.

# Raul Marin

This is another close friend, and he has assisted me in teaching my classes for the Police Bujitsu Club. Raul was also a student of Andries Cane for many years, and the artist for our logo. The part he played was not in the book itself, but in the presentation portion of this course, and as the driver of the vehicle, he put on a good show. Raul has been a great friend for more that 20 years.

# Vera Mendoza

My wonderful wife needs a special thanks for supporting me and giving me the time it took away from us to work on this book, as well as the time to teach classes in between. Being an artist, and a student of martial arts, she has a great eye for arrangement and design in helping me put things together. She also helped edit this book, of which my writing skills have a lot to be desired. You are an inspiration to me, as well as the love of my life. All my Love to her.

With the help from my friends, this book and training course has come together. I believe it will be a great success. One final thanks. I thank <u>God</u> for these wonderful friends, and for them all being a part of my life.

# FOREWARD

As a young boy, I was always fascinated by feats of strength and our many super heroes of the time. I was never too fond of school work and was what I would call an  average student. I guess you could call me more of a doer than a thinker. Not knowing what I may be good at, I tried many sports from grade school on. I was small boned and short in stature but was blessed in being an above average athlete. I first tried track and field and became a very good sprinter and competitive in the other field events.

While in junior high school, I excelled in physical fitness completing record times in sprints, rope climbing, pushups, sit ups, and anything physical I could find. It was here in junior high school that I found a teacher that was very special in my life, Mr. Ben Heron. He was a science teacher who also taught a special class of trampoline and tumbling early in the morning before school started. I took one look at this and knew that I wanted to learn to do this skill. He welcomed me and taught me many things. After a few months, I was doing exhibitions of tumbling and trampoline work at the halftime of basketball games and at other events. I developed a great sense of balance and kinesthetic awareness from tumbling which was a solid basis for excelling in other sports. After a year of tumbling and trampoline training, I was lucky enough to meet the second teacher who had a lasting effect on my life, Mr. Beuler who was the

coach of the swimming and diving team. He had seen me do tumbling and trampoline work and asked me to dive for the swim team at the State meet. I told him that I did not know how to dive, but he said he had seen me tumble and I would be able to learn diving. So I thought, "Why not give it a try?" After being instructed that afternoon on the fine points of diving, I was told the State meet was in two days, so I would have two days to learn how to dive. To my great surprise, I finished second in my first diving competition at state level. After swimming and diving for a few months, I thought I found my sport. I became a speed swimmer and broke multiple records in the 50 and 100 meter events in sev-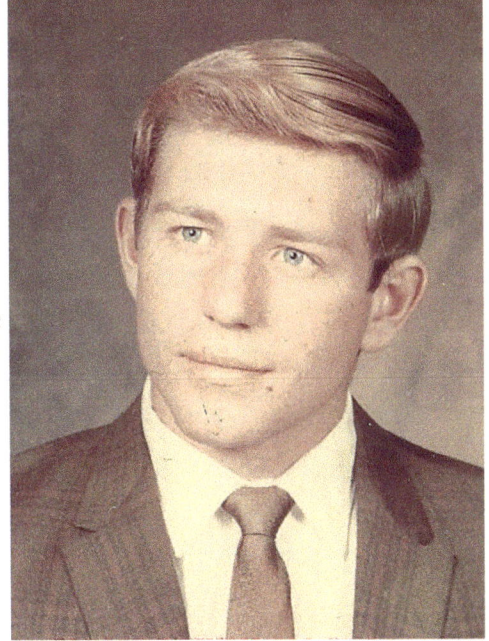

When I got to high school, I found that physical education was all but eliminated, so I tried out for the track and football teams and was good enough to set school and state records. I enjoyed sports but realized that I was not going to be able to make a career of sports, so in my last two years of high school, I worked nights in a hospital and went to school during the day thinking this might be the path I needed to follow in

After high school, I went to Dickinson State University in North Dakota where I enrolled in their nursing program. I had received multiple scholarship offers to play

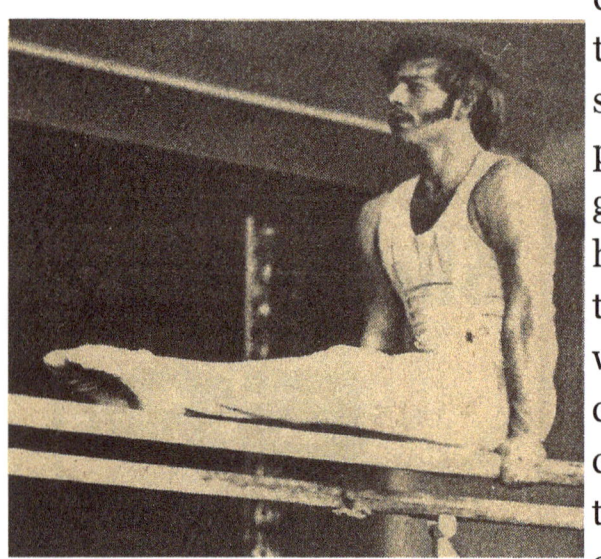

college football but at only 150 pounds, I decided that might not be the path for me to follow but soon after my arrival in college that urge to compete was back. There was a great gymnastics program at the university, and my new roommate had been a gymnast for several years. Again, I thought "Why not give it a try?" As a "walk on" without a scholarship, I made the team and became a gymnast and competed throughout the country and competed in international competitions. Gymnastics developed a even better physical awareness and balance in my life.

I graduated from college and worked only a short time as a nurse in a hospital in North Dakota before the urge to do something more physical, as my life's work hit me, and I knew I had to go. I joined the U.S. Air Force and volunteered for the elite Para Rescue Service. Para Rescue in the Air Force is the equivalent of the other services Special Forces (Army Delta Force, Navy Seal Teams) so needless to say this filled my need for something physical, and I was also able to use my medical training to boot! I thought I had found my niche for life, but as fate would have it, this was not to be. I was injured in a diving accident which eliminated me from the Air Force. After I left the Air force, I was still looking for that physical training that I had been looking for since childhood. I found two things that peaked

I took a dare from a friend to compete in a body building contest, and I found that I could compete, and I made a go of it for a couple of years competing all over the country and won multiple amateur titles. In my last competition, I won Southwest Mr. America .

After several years of moving from state to state while competing in bodybuilding, I had the opportunity to study different styles of martial arts under several different sensei's. While never having the opportunity to really follow up and continue with one specific form, after settling in San Antonio, I was fortunate enough to meet Mr. Andries Cane. I became his student in the American Budo-kan style. Mr. Cane had been a worldwide competitor in Judo and through years of study in Europe and Japan, had studied Judo, Jujitsu, Bujitsu, and Aikido. He had received eleven black belts in these various martial arts. While studying under Mr. Cane, I joined the San Antonio Police Department and quickly realized these martial art skills could be incorporated into police training tactics.

During my development in martial skills, I studied the formal and informal styles. I took special interest in the informal training which was incorporated into training police officers. I had become an instructor with Mr. Cane and after many years working with him, he retired and gave me the honor of taking over the forty years of his lifelong work. I have developed the Police Bujitsu Club, LLC. where his work is still honored, practiced and has been developed into training for police agencies all over the United States through hands on

**YOU CAN MAKE A DIFFERENCE**

# Vehicle Extractions

## This course was written for the

## POLICE BUJITSU CLUB, LLC.
By
Gary G. Albrecht

This course was developed for all law enforcement agencies to safely extract prisoners from vehicles. There are ways to extract persons from a vehicle that allow the officer to have control, whether passive or aggressive persons are involved. Complete control is the secret. At no time should we allow a prisoner or suspect the time to become more aggressive or give them a chance to escape.

Having control over a person does not mean that you have to place them in pain. The control is your positioning, and the positioning of the person involved. A major consideration is placed on your approach to the person in the vehicle. Your control over this person has to be flexible enough to adjust to an escalating situation, such as when a person changes from cooperative to uncooperative or even to violent during the extraction. You may not have time to respond to a sudden change of attitude, unless a fully controlled extraction is used. The best extraction technique is the one in which **NO** repositioning is necessary, and maintaining control is simply a matter of applying the appropriate pressure in response to the level of escalation. Which technique you choose to use during the extraction may vary due to the person's positioning in his or her vehicle or the behavior of the person being extracted.

The techniques used in this course are taught with the officer's safety in mind, and keeping the officer and agency liability to a minimum.

*All rights reserved. No unauthorized reproduction allowed.*

**GARY G. ALBRECHT**

© COPYRIGHT 2009

# INTRODUCTION

In the past, officers have used multiple means of getting persons to exit their vehicles. Some of these methods have proven to cause injury to the person or prisoner extracted, in turn resulting in <u>lawsuits</u>, and some have caused injury to the officers, resulting in time off due to injury.

It appears that the subject of extracting persons from vehicles has <u>not</u> generally been addressed in detail by law enforcement agencies in the United States, other than <u>Felony Stop Situations,</u> where the extraction is with guns drawn and verbal commands used. But, what about the hundreds of thousands of vehicle stops that are <u>not</u> felony stops? As police officers, you know that a vast majority of your arrests come from these type of stops.

Now we look at today's world of modern technology where camera and video capabilities are prevalent. They are on buildings, cell phones, on police vehicles and uniforms, etc. In a situation in which the police officer is trying to do his job by making an arrest, but the arrestee refuses to exit the vehicle as he is told and is not fighting the officer, it can be a tough call. Lets say the officer tries to get the arrestee out of the vehicle by any means he can - pulling, pushing, yanking. The arrestee inside the vehicle is now hanging onto the steering wheel, head rest, and seat belt, but still not exiting the vehicle but not fighting the officer, either. Things seem to escalate at this point. **<u>WHERE DO WE DRAW THE LINE</u>**, AND **<u>WHO DO YOU THINK IS TAKING YOUR PICTURE?</u>** Bystanders could be just observing or possibly taking pictures. As usual, the liability is on you and your department. *"That brutal officer, pulling that poor man or woman out of their own car and using that amount of force......."*

Using these advanced vehicle extraction techniques can help maintain the appearance of a well trained professional, handling a difficult situation. There is no overreacting by the officer, even though the person in the vehicle is resisting arrest. The extraction is accomplished with little or no injury, and the arrest is

# Chapter 1
# Elbow Hyperextension

# The Inner Voice

This portion of the book is something that needs to be addressed, but yet it is hard to explain exactly what it is. What I mean is that most people have experienced it in their life or at least have heard of it. Yes, that _little voice_, _inner voice_, _special feeling,_ or _precognition_ is what tells us that something is wrong or to watch out and be careful. Whatever it tells you, and wherever it comes from, it is something that we need to learn to listen to. Whether you call it a guardian angel, an instinct, or the voice of God himself, this is something that we should learn to listen to. Whatever you want to call it, it is there for a purpose. **YOUR SAFETY**.

I know that you have heard stories of persons that had that inner voice say not to get on that airplane or get in that car, and listened to it. Then shortly after, the plane or car crashed, or something bad happened.

I have heard stories of many officers in the field having that same feeling, or that little voice telling them something is wrong or dangerous. The ones that listened are alive to tell about it. I don't believe it is just luck but that there is something to it that is put out there for our protection.

I am sure this has happened many times in my life, and sometimes I thought, "**Wow**, it was lucky I didn't do that."

I am going to tell you the first time, as a police officer, when this phenomena really came to my attention.

Well, it was late at night in San Antonio, Texas, about 2:30 am or so. The night was warm, and I was a rookie officer working "dog watch". I had been on the police department only a year or so, when I observed a person on a motorcycle break some traffic law. I don't recall the traffic offense that the rider broke to get my attention at this time, but I was going to make the stop. I do remember the biker, because he was flying his colors. The sleeveless dirty, blue jean jacket with the name "BANDIDOS" on the back, and what was suppose to be a white t-shirt under it. I remember him wearing dirty blue jeans, and black boots, and a helmet. The helmet was a state law at that time, but it was black and skinned up with deep gouges and scrapes on it. The motorcycle of course was a Harley, black in color, and a lot of chrome on the engine as well as other parts, such as the long kick stand and the mirrors on each side of the handle bars.

I lit up my patrol car's lights using the emergency lights, which squeaked and made lane when I had hit my lights. He pulled to the right, across the outside lane to the side of the road where the curb was.

With him being a motorcycle gang member, a big guy at that, night time, not many people around, and not asking for cover, with all this in mind, I was a little uneasy making the stop. Let's put it this way, I was a little nervous. I told myself, "Well this feeling is just because I am a rookie, and it was natural to feel this way."

As the biker comes to a stop on the side of the road, I see his feet come down and can see him looking side to side. He then reaches back with his left foot, kicking down the long kick stand. He never looks back at me but tries to see what I am doing by watching through his mirrors, and by moving the handlebars back and forth to get a good view.

This is the time that "little voice" from within me says, "There is something wrong; it's just not right. Don't approach the bike like you usually do". I opened my door, and left it open and then went back around to the rear of my patrol car, and approached from the right side , while watching the biker. I took my time and watched around as I approached. I could see the biker was watching his left mirror moving the front fork back and forth. The sound of the bike still running helped my approach from being heard. I got almost next to the biker when I asked him for his drivers license and insurance. The biker jumped as I spoke, not expecting me on that side of the bike. I could see that he was nervous, but what the heck, so was I. I asked him to turn off his bike and step over to the sidewalk. I could see he was uncomfortable, and he hesitated, then he looked around a few times before complying. With a good police tactical stance, I observed him closely as he pulled out a large black folding wallet on the end of a chain, and he gave me his drivers license. I checked him on the information channel since we did not have computers in our cars at that time. The biker came back with warrants, so I placed him in handcuffs right away. When searching him, I found some cocaine in his inside jacket pocket as well. We did not have protective cages in our patrol cars at this time, so I sat him down at the curb while I called for the wrecker. The wrecker just took a short time getting there, and I barely had time to get all his information down on my paperwork.

When it came time for the wrecker to put the straps on the bike and take it to the pound, I saw that the left handle bar was different then the right. The left handle bar was about six inches longer and was made with a hinge toward the end of it. I looked carefully at the mirror on the left side, and I saw cross hairs marked into the mirror like on a rifle scope.

I was able to open the hinge and found a loaded shot gun shell, chambered in the handle bar. This was for all purposes a shot gun that aimed back behind the rider through the end of the handle bar. After the biker was placed in my patrol car, and we were on the way downtown, the biker stated he was going to kill me as I approached him on the left side when I got close. **But,** I screwed the entire thing up by approaching on the other side. *Thank That Little Voice.*

# ANOTHER TRUE STORY

*I would like to give you another vehicle extraction story that had happened to another officer that worked for the San Antonio Police Department. This story happened to an officer who we will call Officer L.*

Officer L. was new on the force, but he was a born warrior who chose Law Enforcement as his career. It didn't take him long to build a reputation for efficiency and dependability, even before he faced his greatest challenge.

It happened one evening just before dark when a speeding car rocketed past him; radar showed the vehicle well over the posted limit.

With his emergency lights on, siren wailing, he was soon close behind the speeder. The vehicle slowed and pulled over to the curb, and Officer L. stopped about 10 feet behind the speeder.

He opened his patrol car door, and stepped out, picking up his hat and citation book. Officer L. began walking toward the driver's side until he was almost to the back bumper, when suddenly, without knowing why, he jumped sideways behind the car. As he did so, the driver twisted his body, swung his right arm out of the window and fired two rounds where Officer L. should have been.

Officer L. pulled his weapon, firing through the back window, killing the gunman.

From that moment on, he told every officer he should pay attention and respond to their feelings, and listen to that voice — **INSIDE.**

# Hand Positioning for Vehicle Extractions

While these vehicle extractions are being taught, hand positioning is a very important part of this process in order to achieve maximum control. The hand positioning is shown separately so you can get the form that is necessary to accomplish your extraction with full control.

1A      2A      3A

Figure 1A. Position the arm for a hyperextension position. The first part of the position is to place your left hand fingers down over the top of the prisoner's wrist turning the his palm forward and his arm extended straight to his side.

Figure 2A. and Figure 3A. Bring the right arm over the top of the suspect's arm while keeping the palm forward and the arm extended.

4A      5A      6A

Figure 4A. Position your right arm over the suspect's arm with your fingers down in front of his arm, allowing your elbow also to pass over his arm, pulling it back toward your chest.

Figure 5A. As you are pulling the arm back to your chest, push the suspects's arm forward so the pressure of your body is behind the elbow. Keep the arm tight to your chest by pulling back with your left hand and pulling the arm tight to your chest with your entire right arm.

Figure 6A. By keeping the suspect's arm tight to your chest, then turning back toward your left side, you will hyperextend the suspect's arm.
**(This is where caution is needed.)**

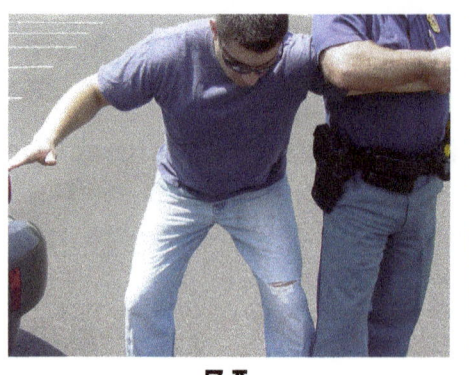 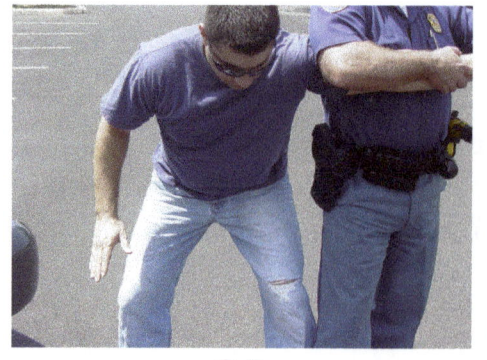 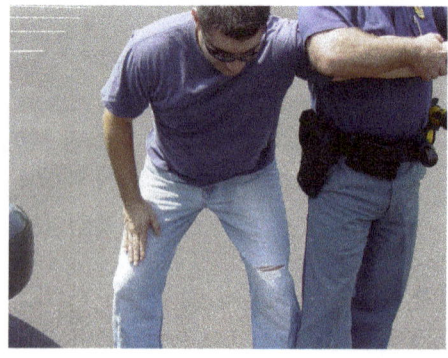

7A          8A          9A

Figure 7A.,8A.,and 9A. The caution here is twofold. First is in practice: (1) When performing these techniques, there is a great deal of pressure put on the suspect's elbow. Remembering that the actor or "uke" in practice is allowing you to do these techniques on him. <u>**DO NOT HURT HIM OR HER**</u>...... The hyperextension on the elbow is increased as you turn back to your left, and the faster you turn the more pressure you apply. In practice, be aware of the actor you are working with. If the pressure on his elbow begins to hurt, he is instructed to <u>**TAP**</u> . The tap comes when the actor slaps his leg, chest, arm or wherever, to let you know the pressure is causing pain and for you to let up on the pressure you are applying. (2) When performed on the street in real action, your control is still needed. These types of hyperextensions may be done passively or aggressively as needed. You are the one in control, and the control comes from the speed of your turn. Reacting too quickly and too fast may result in injury to the actor.

A little saying goes through my head that I have to bring up. "**<u>BE HERE NOW</u>.**" The saying was told to me by my sensei and his wife. (Andries Cane and Renae Cane) The meaning is something all officers should understand and practice. To explain this little phrase is simple; <u>***don't***</u> be thinking of what's going to happen later - a date your going on late, a text you have to send, a coffee break, or whatever. Be thinking about the task at hand. Your attention has to be there at that time and place. The second you get lax, you may find some unwelcome surprises in your life . These are surprises that we don't need in police work, and it could mean your life. Have your attention and focus be totally locked on what your doing at that time.

# Vehicle Approach

After you have made the vehicle stop, and hopefully, you have been able to call in your location and descriptions of color, number of occupants, and whatever information you are able to give, then it is time for your approach.

*REMEMBER THAT INNER VOICE.*

1B      2B      3B      4B

Figure 1B. On your approach, use good tactics, keep alert and **" Be Here Now"**. Make your observations as you approach the vehicle in the most appropriate way.

Figure 2B, and 3B. When you get to the rear of the vehicle, make sure the trunk of the vehicle is secure by lifting on the trunk lid or back hatch.

Figure 4B. Keep your body bladed, as in an interview stance, so you are prepared to draw your weapon.

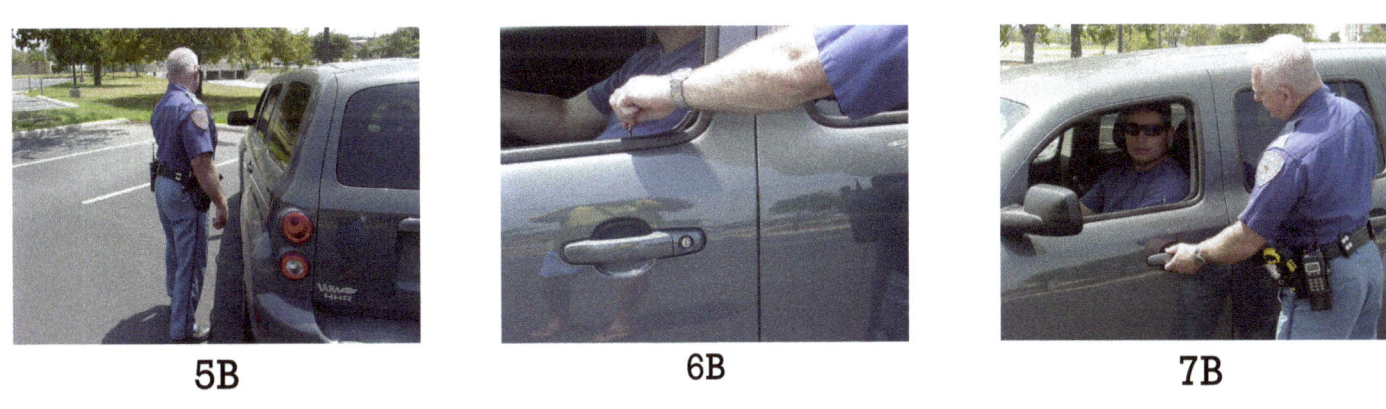

5B      6B      7B

Figure 5B. Keep your body close to the vehicle as you are approaching the driver. This will make you a harder target if the driver should attempt to shoot from the window.

Figure 6B. If you are going to have this driver exit the vehicle, when possible, unlock the door as you speak to the driver.

Figure 7B. After asking the driver to step out of his vehicle, control the opening of the door, allow him to open it, or you open it for him.

# Extraction I
# Elbow Hyperextension

After the approach, the next decision you need to make is which extraction you will use to remove the person from the vehicle. One of the easiest ones to use with great control is the "Elbow Hyperextension Extraction". This technique can be used as a passive extraction or an aggressive one in case of escalation. The technique does not change from passive to aggressive by changing the position of hands or feet. The only real change is in the attitude of the person you are extracting. That is where passive turns to aggressive, but still under your control.

1C    2C    3C

When you have determined that the extraction you are going to use is the elbow hyperextension, (Figure 1C), give yourself plenty of working room. Allow the door to open completely, leaving yourself a complete view of suspect, while making sure that there are no weapons, and no one else to interfere.

Figure 2C. Control of the extraction starts here when ordering the suspect to put his left arm outside the door.

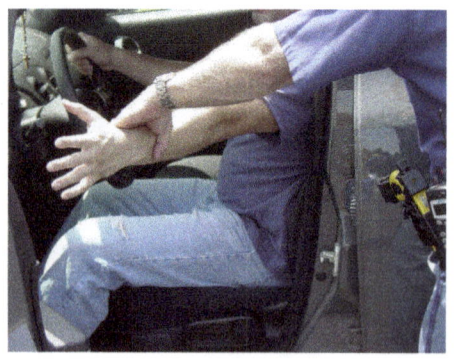 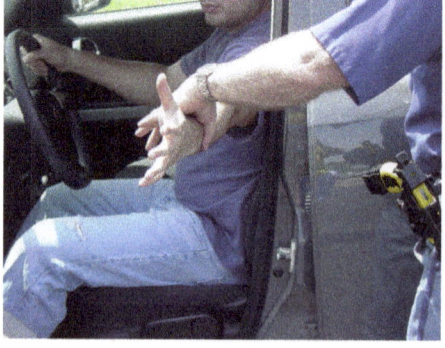 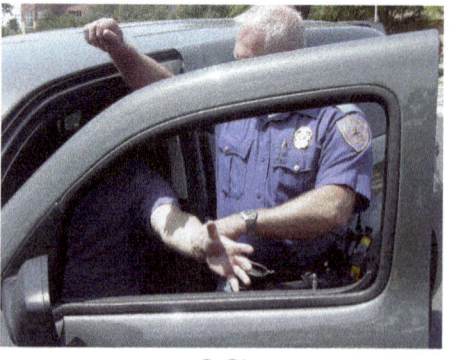

4C    5C    6C

Figure 3C. When the arm is placed outside the door, you want to make sure the arm is fully extended, not allowing it to bend at the elbow, or allowing it to move forward

Figure 4C. And 5C. Now place your left hand over the top of his wrist, and grab his wrist so that your fingers are in the front. This position will allow you to control the subject's arm so that his palm and forearm stay in a forward position, and so the arm is fully extended. Pulling his arm to a fully extended position, also causes your suspect to become unbalanced. When the arm is pulled out to the side of the subject, his shoulder also extends which causes an immediate body tilt to that side.

Figure 6C. Bring your body in so that your right hip slides in behind the subjects elbow as it is extended out of the doorway. This will allow you to position your body between the subject's body and his elbow. You need to be in this position to allow the suspect's arm to hyperextend as pressure is being applied while pulling back on the wrist. You will notice that your right arm is up above the subject's arm, being placed over the top.

7C  8C  9C

Figure 7C, 8C, and 9C. The right hand comes over the top fingers, down with the palm facing you. Place your right hand on the subject's wrist and forearm, pulling the arm tight to your body. Your back should be up against the post of the car. This position will give your back support and turning power that will allow you to stay in an upright posture for better controlled movement .

10C

Figure 10C. This shows the position of both hands on the suspect's arm, with the back being supported against the post of the vehicle. <u>**NOTICE: The officer's back is straight, and he is not leaning over to control the arm.**</u> At this time, you need to pull the arm forward in front of you and place your body behind the suspect's elbow for control.

**11C**

Figure 11C. This view allows you to see how much of your back is in the vehicle. This will give you the support that is needed using the post of the vehicle if the situation should escalate. The feet are placed so the left foot is back to allow the officer to turn to the left side as soon as the suspect starts to exit the vehicle.

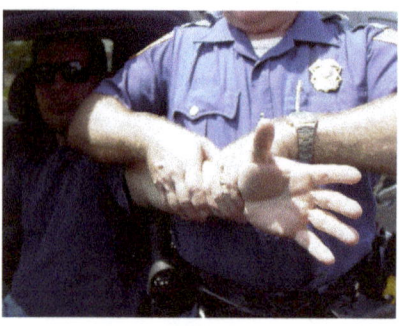

**12C** **13C** **14C**

Figure 12C., 13C., and 14C. The extending of the suspect's arm is important, as this allows the right side of your body to be placed behind the elbow. This allows the hyperextension of the suspect's elbow, and allows you to position your back against the post of the vehicle for support. **NOTICE: The palm and forearm of the suspect are still in a forward possession.**

**15C** **16C** **17C**

Figures 15C. This picture shows the start of the progression from the start of the turn by the officer which places the suspect in a hyperextension causing pain and the need to comply.

Figure 16C. The officer has turned about an eighth of a turn back to his left, increasing the pressure on the suspect's arm. The suspect at this point will need to lean forward in order to exit the vehicle.

Figure 17C. The officer has turned almost a full quarter turn, and the subject has to step out of the vehicle as fast as he can to keep up with the turn of the officer. Slow down if needed to prevent any injury, giving him ample time to exit his vehicle.

 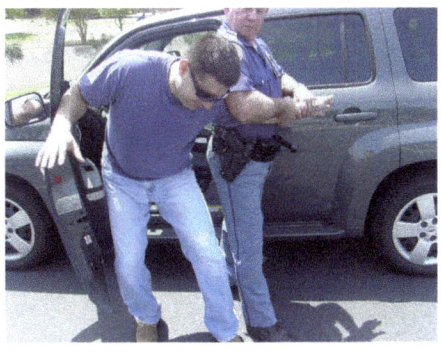 

18C   19C   20C

Figure 18C. Turn beyond the quarter of a turn and allow the suspect to exit the vehicle. Make sure that his feet are not behind yours. Keeping the suspect's arm tight to your body as you turn, assures you that he will keep up with your turning speed.

Figure 19C and 20C. As the officer turns and keeps the suspect's arm tight to him, he will have to reposition his feet to increase the turning radius slightly.

  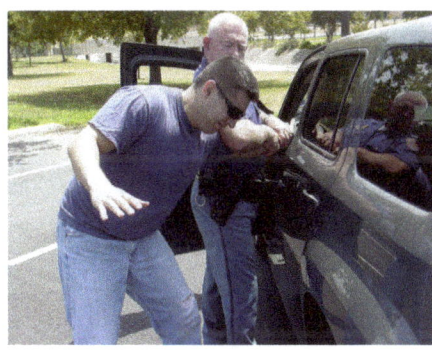

21C   22C   23C

Figures 21C, 22C, and 23C. The officer has turned almost facing the vehicle and has allowed himself plenty of room to turn, and has positioned his feet in order to allow him to keep the pressure on the arm. The suspect's palm is now flat up against the vehicle.

 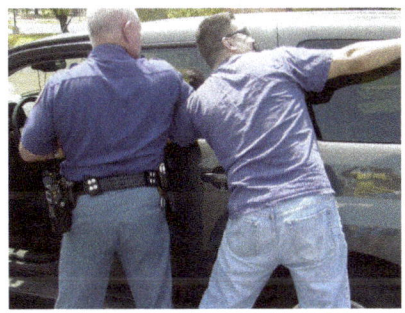 

24C   25C   26C

Figures 24C, 25C, and 26C. The officer has now turned just past parallel with the vehicle. This will make the suspect's body press tightly against the vehicle, giving him no room to bend over, or turn in either direction.

27C          28C          29C

Figure 27C. Keep the hyperextension on the suspect's arm turned past parallel with the vehicle, and watch the suspect to make sure he is tight against the vehicle.

Figure 28C. Release the right hand from the front of the arm, and maintain control by pressing the suspect's hand and arm close to the vehicle while not allowing his arm to bend.

Figure 29C. Prepare for the upward strike using your right elbow.

## NOTE:

*Placing a prisoner in a handcuffing position has always been a problem for officers, especially when the subject that is being placed in handcuffs is not cooperating. A little understanding of the anatomy is all that is needed to gain control over your suspect. The path of least resistance in this case is placing the arm in the weakest anatomical position. To explain where this position is on the arm, is the easy part, but to get your suspect in this position is the technique that has to be explained.*

*The weakest anatomical position is when the arm is extended out to the side perpendicular to the body, and the arm is bent at a right angle, with the arm bent upward or downward. This position eliminates the larger muscles from assisting the arm when they are needed in an attempt to pull away from the officer during the handcuffing.*

*There are four short muscles that originate on the scapula and pass around the shoulder where their tendons fuse together to form the Rotator Cuff. These four muscles are the Supraspinatus, Infraspinatus, Teres Minor, and the Subscapularis. Rotation of the upper arm is accomplished by these four muscles collectively, and all form the Rotator Cuff holding the shoulder in place and stabilizing the shoulder.*

*Getting your suspect to this position will now be explained, as we put the suspect into the proper positions in the upcoming photos.*

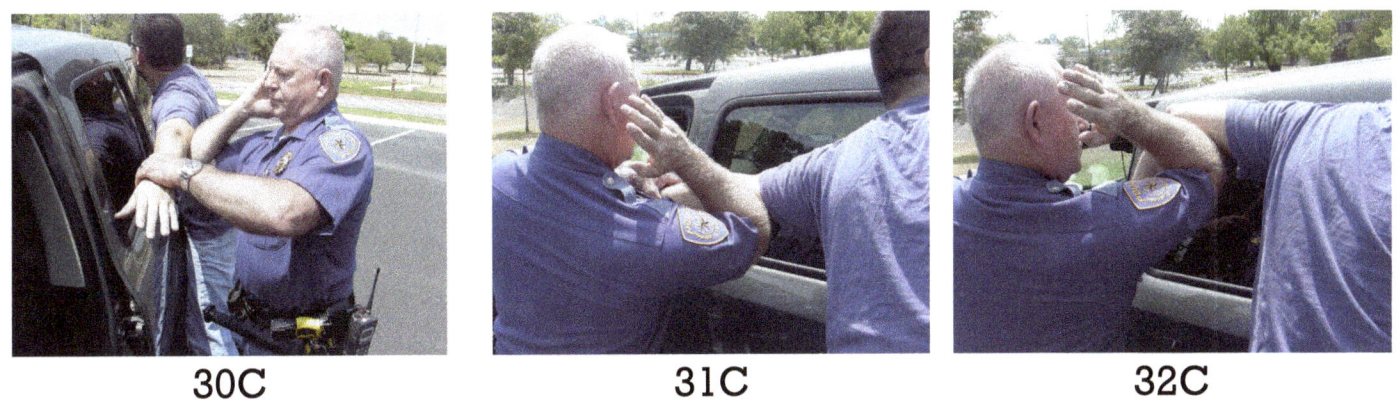

30C  31C  32C

Figure 30C.and 31C. Place the right elbow just above the elbow joint, not to injure the joint of the suspect, but to bend the arm, and place it into the anatomical weak position that was previously explained.

Figure 32C. Allow the suspect's arm to bend as soon as the pressure is placed under the elbow area, while keeping the arm extended perpendicular from the body.

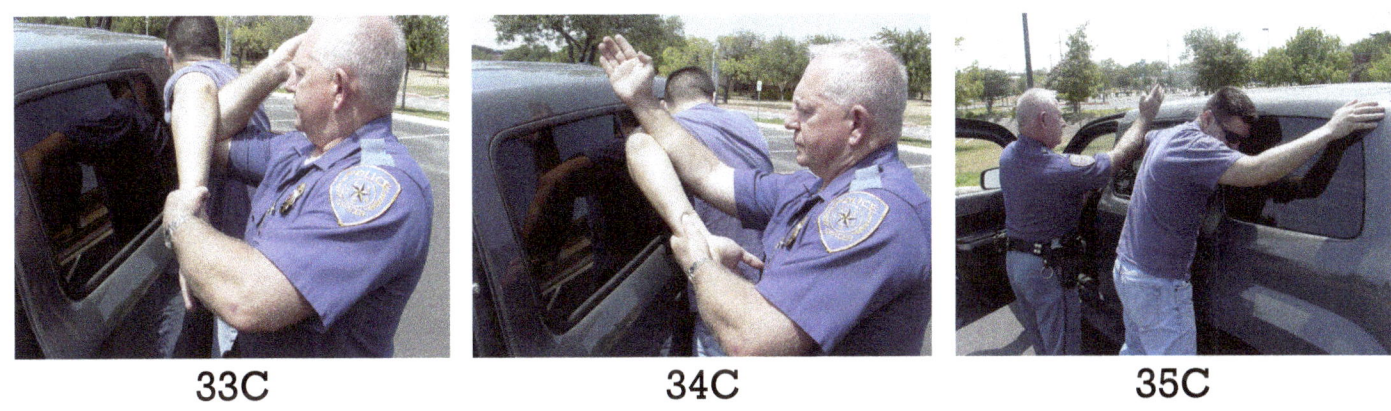

33C  34C  35C

Figure 33C. As your right elbow is pushing upward, the left hand assists in placing the suspect's arm in a right angle. Your elbow should extend forward under the suspect's arm until it is in the right angle position.

Figure 34C. and 35C. Keep your arm in contact with the suspect's arm, and extend your right arm as in a karate chopping position. This will use the weakest position of his arm to allow you to rotate the suspect's arm back far enough, not to injure him, but to allow the pressure on his arm to rotate him slightly forward. Keep him up against the vehicle, with his arm still at a right angle, and prepare his arm to be placed in a locking position.

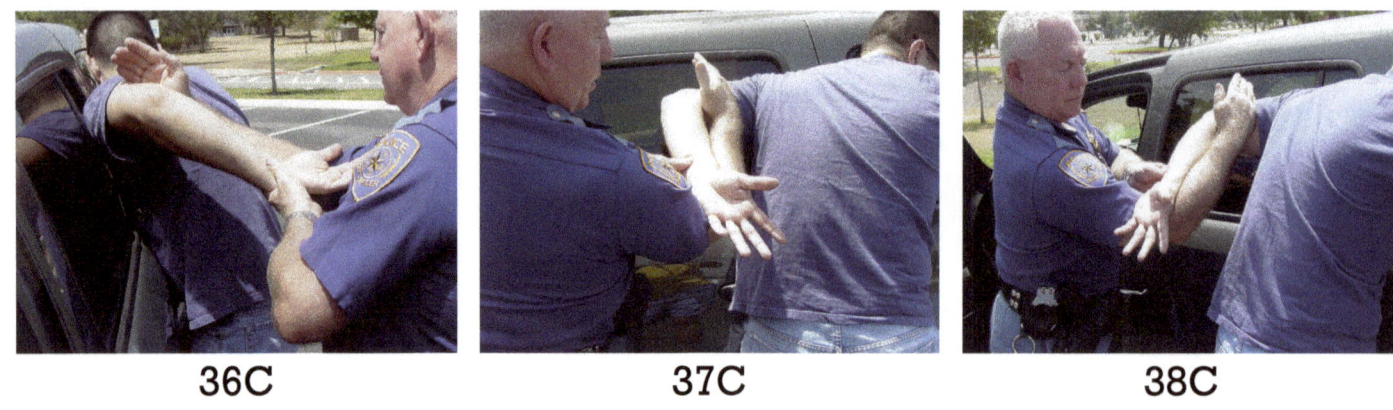

36C  37C  38C

Figure 36C. and 37C. Allow your right arm to extend back while still placing pressure on the arm with the side of your right hand, thus giving you room to have your left hand slide the suspect's hand and arm over the top of your right forearm.

Figure 38C. Make sure the suspect's hand and arm are over the top of your forearm as you release your left hand.

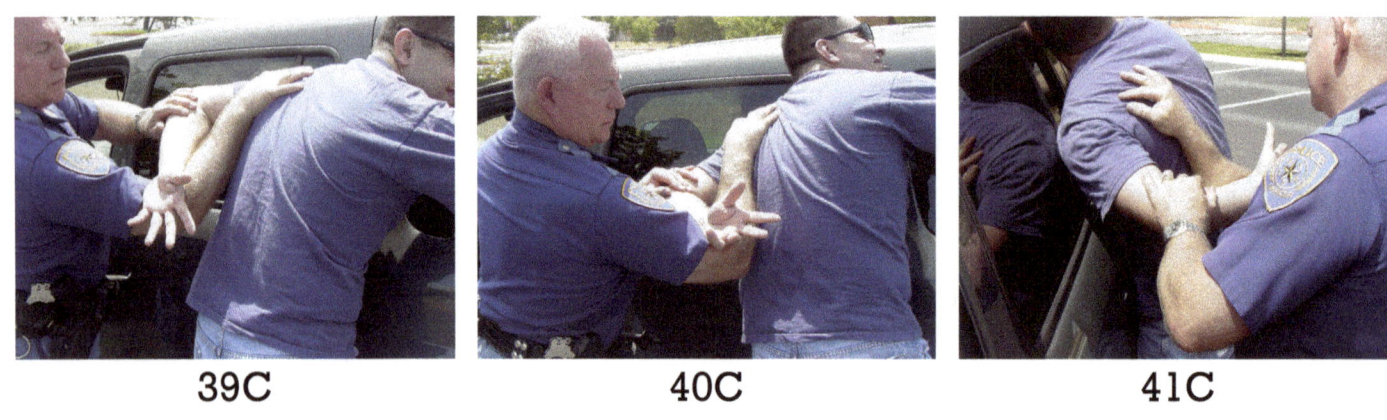

39C  40C  41C

Figure 39C. After releasing your left hand, place it at the elbow of the suspect for control, while your right hand turns over on the back of his shoulder palm down.

Figure 40C. Apply some pressure on the suspect's left elbow. Allow it to come down from the perpendicular position assuring the suspect's arm is locked over the top of yours, as your right arm bends forward to his back. This will lock his arm in place, not allowing him to be able to push downward in order to escape.

Figure 41C. Keep the suspect pushed forward against the vehicle with your right hand on the suspect's back, and your right elbow bent, locking his arm in so he can not push his hand down. Your left hand continues to put some pressure on his elbow, so the suspect's arm can not be brought to the side and forward.

42C　　　　　　　　　　　　　　43C

Figure **42C**. From the left side, watching the stance of the officer, the right foot is forward and the left is back. This foot position allows the officer to keep pressure on the suspect's back, keeping him forward against the vehicle. This also allows the officer control of the suspect's left leg should he attempt to turn back to the left. If this should occur, which is very unlikely, the officer should bend his right knee on the back or the side of the suspect's left knee which will take him straight down.

Figure **43C**. From the right side, again observe the officer's stance with the right leg forward and the left leg back. He keeps the suspect up against the vehicle with his right arm for control.

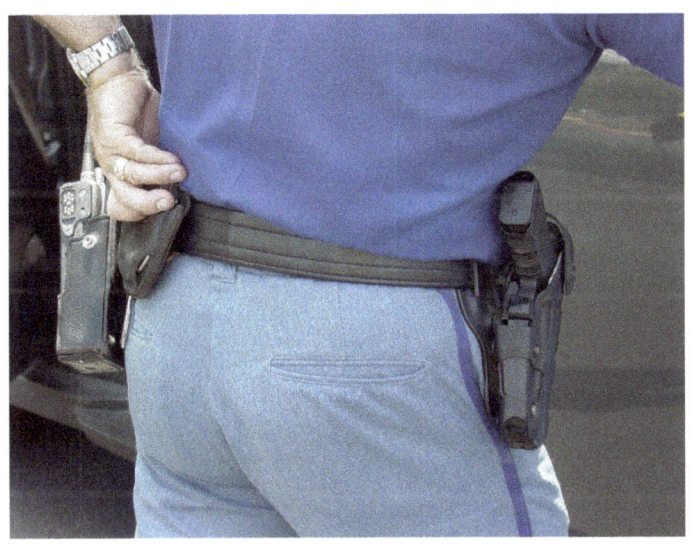 

44C　　　　　　　　　　　　　　45C

Figure **44C**. and **45C**. Pushing against the suspect's back with your right hand and keeping his arm locked over the top of your right arm, allows you to release completely with your left hand to remove your handcuffs from your left side.

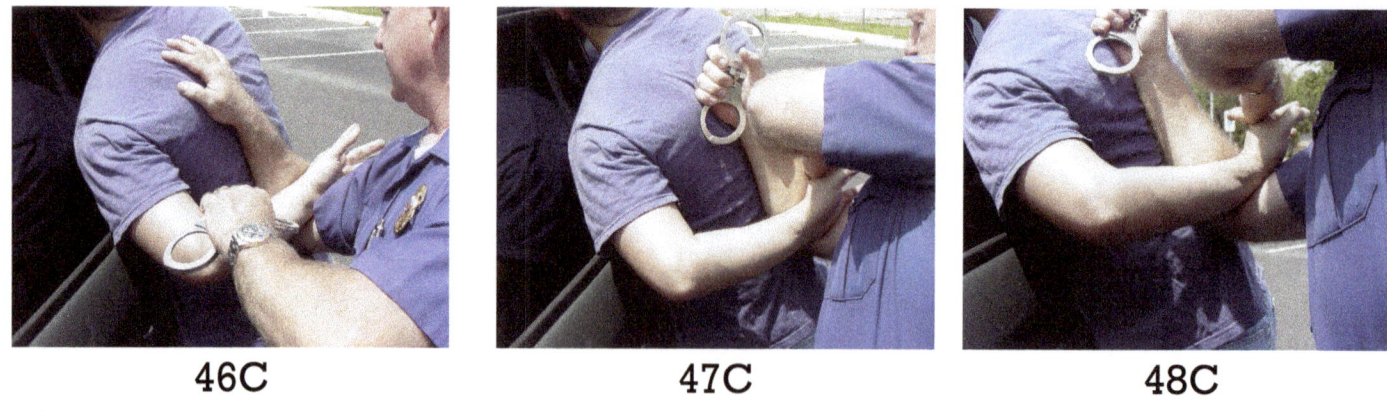

46C  47C  48C

Figure **46C**. After drawing your handcuffs with your left hand, they are brought over the suspect's left arm, while still maintaining in control of the suspect's arm.

Figure **47C**. The handcuffs are passed to your right hand, as your left hand moves to gain control over the suspect's left hand.

Figure **48C**. Reach across to gain control of the suspect's left hand by using a finger-lock.

49C  50C  51C

Figure **49C**. When grabbing the suspect's left hand for control, the palm of your left hand is facing his back. You will place your hand palm to palm on his, while grabbing two to three fingers. This depends on your hand size in comparison to the suspect's.

Figure **50C**. When grabbing the fingers of the suspect, it is important to keep his hand in a flat position and to grab deep onto his hand. Grabbing deep means when your fingers grab his, you are __*not*__ grabbing just the ends of his fingers, but as close to the **web of the fingers** as it is possible, for maximum control.

Figure **51C**. When the finger control is accomplished, you slip your right arm out from under the suspect's left arm. You will maintain control with the finger lock and the pressure you apply with your left forearm against the suspect's left shoulder. The handcuffs are in your right hand and able to be moved in any direction to accomplish handcuffing.

52C  53C  54C

Figure 52C. With the control on the suspect's hand, now move the suspect's hand back toward you away from his body. This space will allow you to place the handcuffs around his wrist.

Figures 53C. and 54C. Press the handcuffs on the suspect's wrist, while still controlling the hand, making sure the cuffs lock.

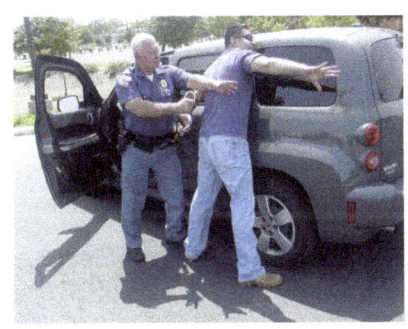  

55C  56C  57C

Figures 55C. and 56C. Now that the handcuff is on the suspect's left wrist, continue to hold the cuff in your left hand, and direct the suspect to give you his right hand.

Figure 57.C Take another finger control lock with two or more fingers on the suspect's right hand, as his arm is brought back toward you.

  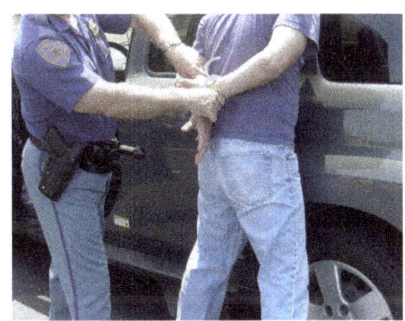

58C  59C  60C

Figures 58C. and 59C. Take control of the suspect's hand, bringing it back far enough to allow placing the right hand in the cuff.

Figure 60C. When placing his right hand in the cuff, bring his hand away from his body if possible, allowing you enough room for the cuff to close, without snagging any clothing.

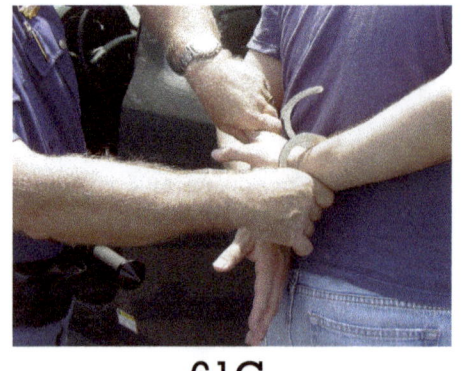  

61C        62C        63C

Figures 61C, and 62C. Press the handcuff onto the right wrist. You can see that the bottom of the cuff was placed **on the left hand first** so that there is no extra turning of the suspect's wrist necessary to complete the cuffing when the right hand is brought across.

Figure 63C. Secure the cuff to the tightness required so the suspect can not slip out of the cuff, but allowing for circulation.

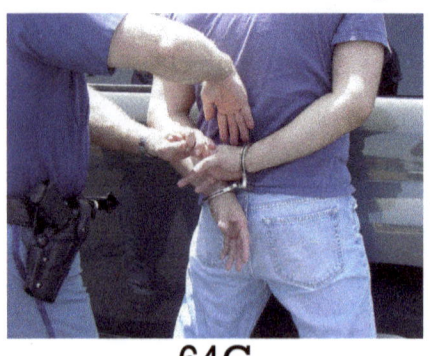  

64C        65C        66C

Figure 64C. After the hand is handcuffed, maintain control with the finger lock. For better control, place your right hand with the palm toward you, up against the back of the suspect so you can reach behind the cuffs.

Figure 65C. Reach behind the cuff with your right hand to the left hand of the sus-

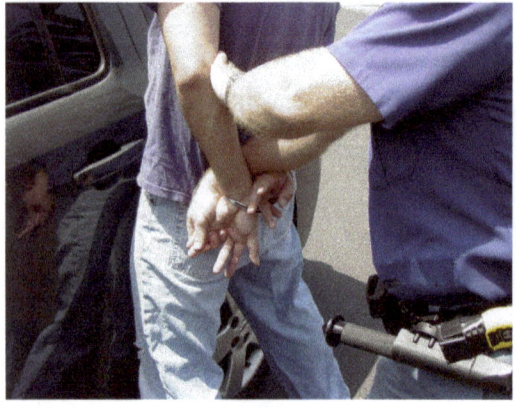

Figures 66C, and 67C. When your right hand has reached the side of the suspect's left hand, you grasp his ring finger and the little finger together. At this point, the amount of pressure needed to keep complete control is minimal. When the fingers are lifted back up toward the cuffs, the amount of pressure you apply at this time depends on the amount of resistance the suspect will give you.

67C

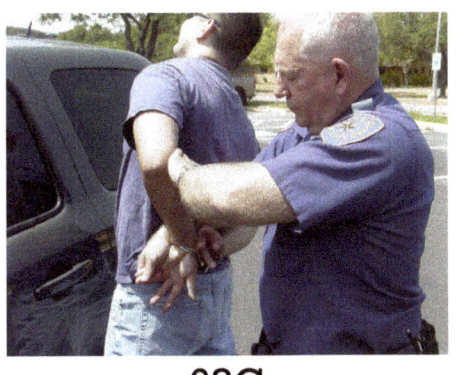
68C

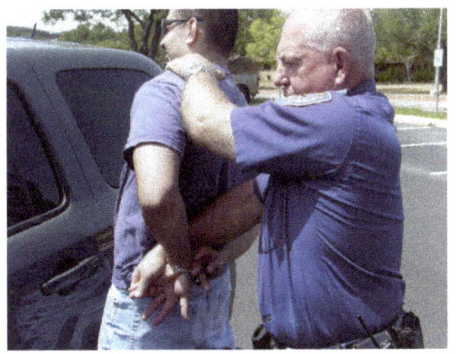
69C

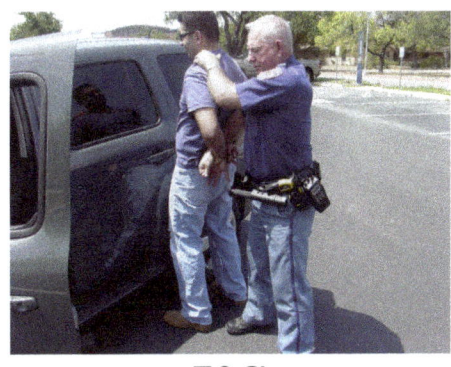
70C

Figure **68C**. Apply pressure to the little finger and the ring finger with your right hand by lifting the fingers up and to the side for control in moving the suspect. Remember, the pressure on the fingers is sideways not back. Pulling the fingers back allows the hold to be less effective. Some people have a great amount of flexibility in their fingers and bending them back may not have an effect.

Figure **69C**. After the fingers are gripped correctly, move your left hand to the suspect's left upper shoulder area. Placing your hand on the shoulder in this fashion gives you better control, and prevents the suspect from throwing his head back into your face.

Figure **70C**. Now you are ready to move your suspect. The first movement should be your left leg stepping out to the left side as you turn your body and the suspect at the same time. Guide the suspect by using his left shoulder to steer him in the direction you want him to go.

## Takedown After Handcuffing

1D

2D

Figures **1D**, and **2D**. After the handcuffing, guide the suspect away from the vehicle by standing him to an upright position and pulling him slightly back. Step back so you are able to move the suspect to his left in a circle. This keeps him off balance enough so you maintain maximum control.

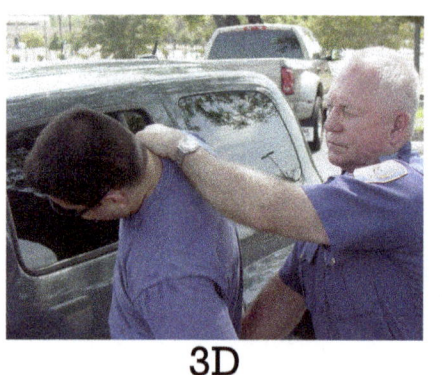 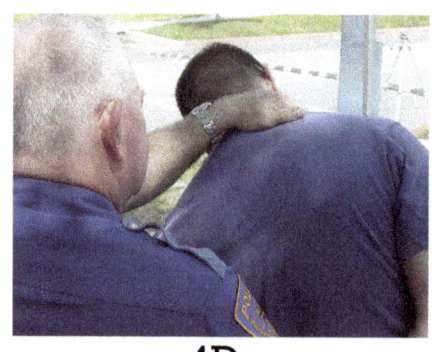 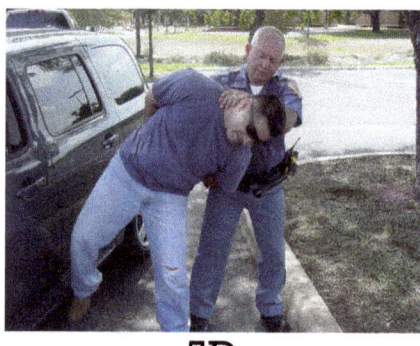

3D      4D      5D

Figure 3D, and 4D. Moving the suspect into a circular position for a quick takedown requires you to have a little more control over the suspect. This control is gained by moving the left hand to the right side of the suspect's neck and placing it on the suspect's upper back next to his neck. This will start a body tilt to the suspect's left and lock the left hip, which gives you the control you want.

Figure 5d. Stepping back with your left foot about 90 degrees while turning the suspect, will set him off-balance onto the left leg.

6D      7D      8D

Figure 6D. Turning the suspect an entire 180 degrees from the vehicle will again require the officer to move his left foot even farther forward to maintain his balance, as well as the suspect's.

Figure 7D. Control of the suspect is important at this time so he doesn't go forward onto his face. Instruct and let him put his left knee down on the ground for his support. This will prevent you from having all of his weight pulling you down. Pulling back with your left hand will center him to allow the left knee to go to the ground and keep the weight from being transferred forward.

Figure 8D. Still maintain control over the suspect's hand not so much by lifting the fingers here but back on the side of the hand, giving more support to the suspect in letting him down easily to the ground. Your left hand is still on his right side, also being used for support.

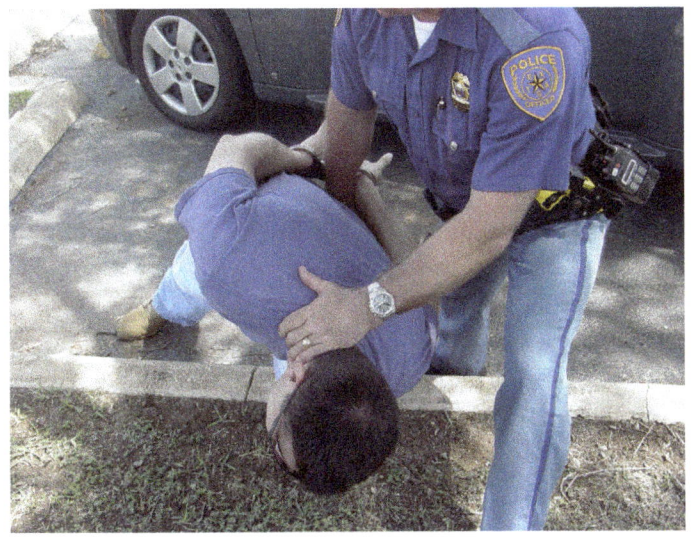
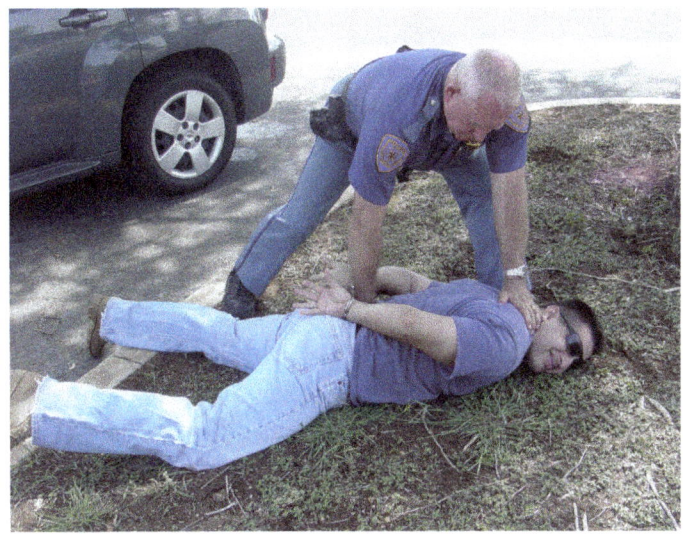

9D

10D

Figure 9D. Make sure that you stand forward giving the suspect the support necessary to lay him onto the ground. Keeping the left hand across on the right side of the suspect's upper back will position his body to be at a slight angle. This will turn his head to the right, causing him to lay on his left shoulder first when touching the ground.

Figure 10D. After he is in a prone position on the ground, keep his head turned away from you while your right hand still has control over the suspect's hands.

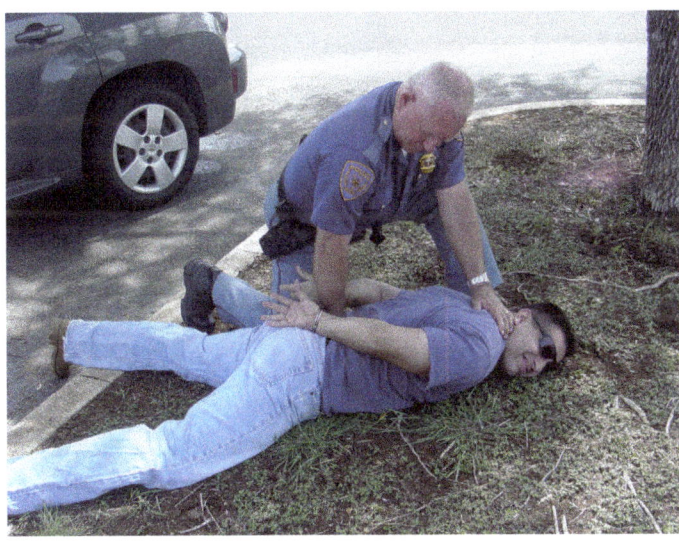
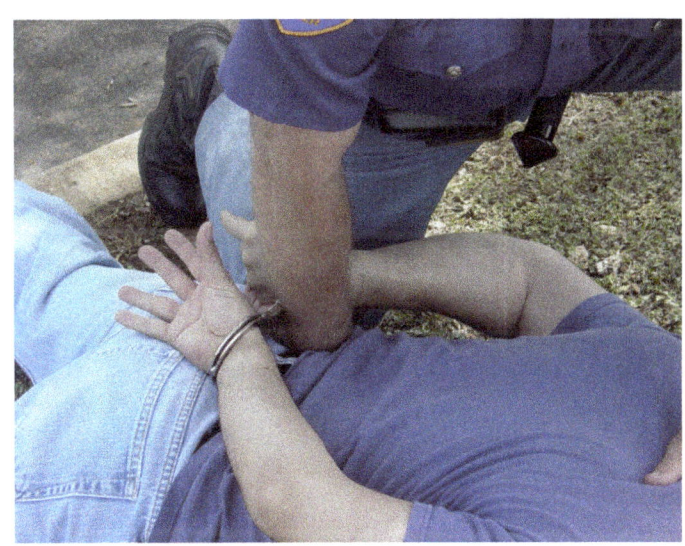

11D

12D

Figures 11D. and 12D. Kneeling down with your right knee, along the suspect's left side, will prevent you from having to bend over to ease any stress on your back, and keep your balance.

# Chapter 2
# Figure Four Lapel grab

# Figure Four Lapel Grab Exit, Ext. II

The vehicle exit that you are about to learn is a figure four lock on the arm as the name suggests. This extraction is used when the suspect is semi-cooperative. This is a very powerful move. The arm of the suspect will be placed in a locking position that places a lot of pressure on the elbow of the person being extracted. The move allows the officer to extract the person with minimal effort. Like all joint manipulation techniques, caution should be used when the lock is placed on the suspect's arm. Moving too fast, or being a little too forceful may result in injury to the suspect. Using a minimal amount of force to get the job done while maintaining control over the suspect, is your ultimate goal.

  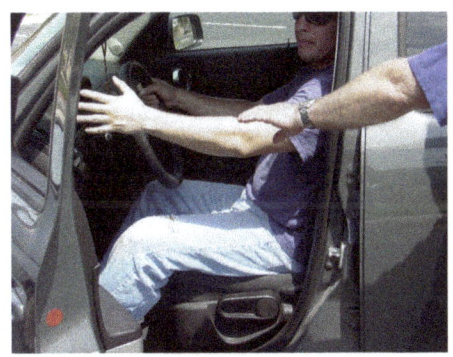

1E    2E    3E

Figure 1E. Make sure you can get to the suspect by unlocking and opening the vehicle door. Even when you ask the suspect to step out of his vehicle, control the vehicle door.

Figure 2E. Take control early by advising the suspect to extend his left arm out to the side. The body posture of the officer is at a bladed stance, keeping his weapon side away from the open door.

Figure 3E. When taking control of the suspect's arm, reach out with your left hand, reaching over the top of the suspect's arm, with your palm down.

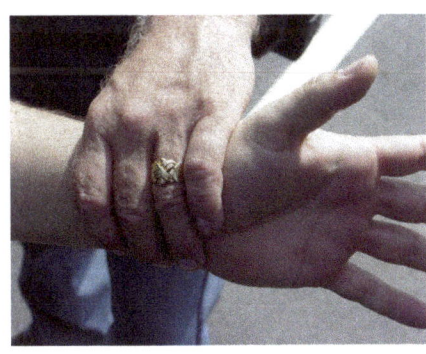

Figure 4E. The position of your left hand should be over the top of the suspect's wrist. Grip the wrist to keep control so the wrist and arm of the suspect remains forward until you step in. The suspect's arm should be in an extended position, out to the side or a right angle to his body, **NOT** bending at the elbow.

4E

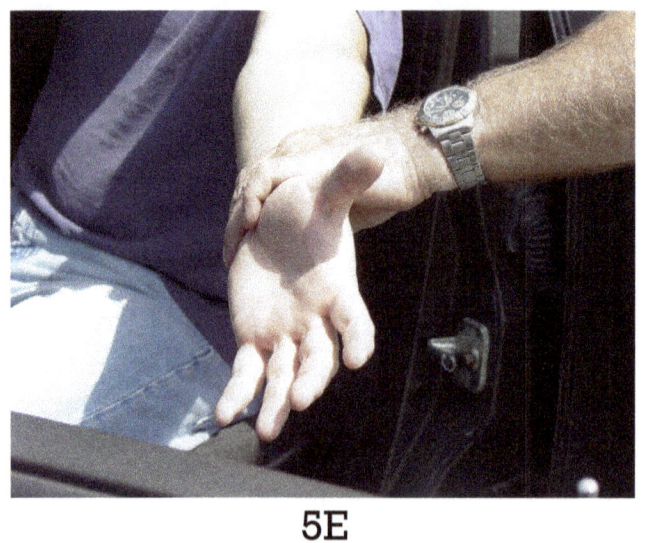
5E

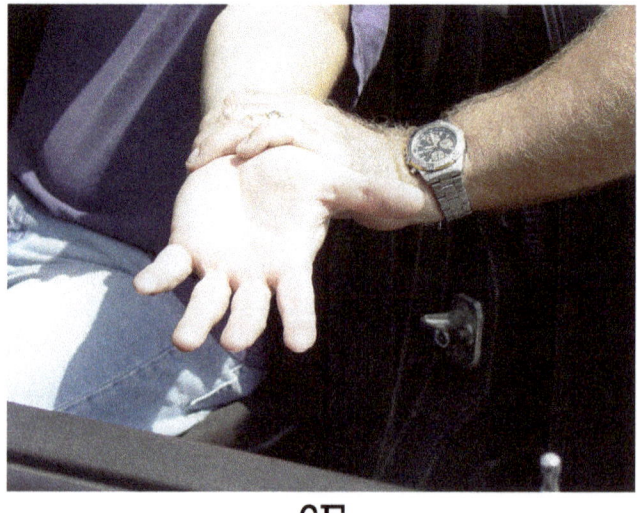
6E

Figures 5E. and 6E. After your grip is secure, rotate the suspect's wrist back in order to position his forearm in an upward position.

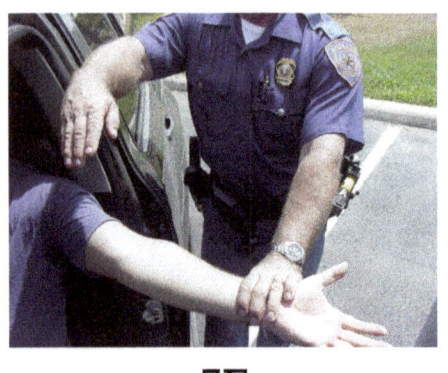
7E

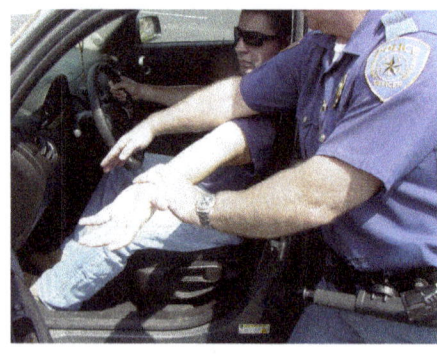
8E

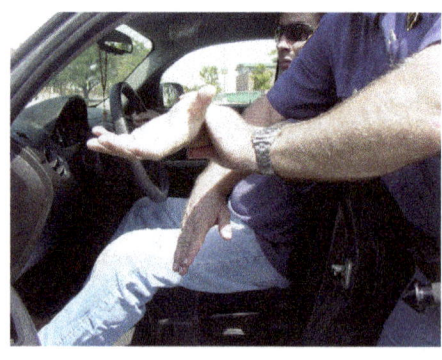
9E

Figure 7E. After the suspect's palm is in an upward position, your right hand reaches over the upper arm of the suspect. Simultaneously, your right hand reaches forward as your right leg also comes forward.

Figure 8E. The right arm of the officer reaches over the bicep area. It is important that his arm stays over the upper arm as it starts to wrap around under the suspect's arm. At this point, a slight pulling out to the side of the suspect's arm will help straighten the arm, making it easier and giving you more room to wrap your arm over the top.

Figure 9E. When your elbow is just past the suspect's arm, it bends down and under. Also, observe that your right leg is forward by the time you start to wrap your arm under the suspect's arm. Maintain balance and proper posture for the lifting leverage needed to do this figure four correctly. The officer's back is straight and not bent forward.

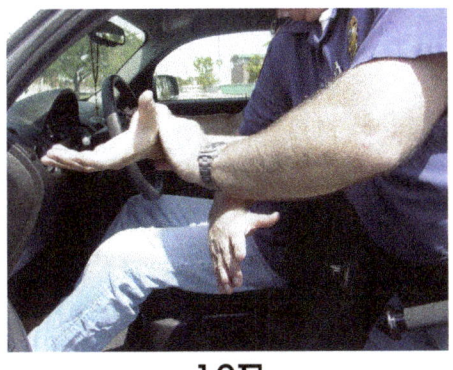 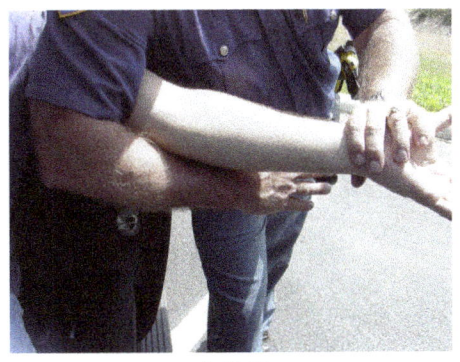 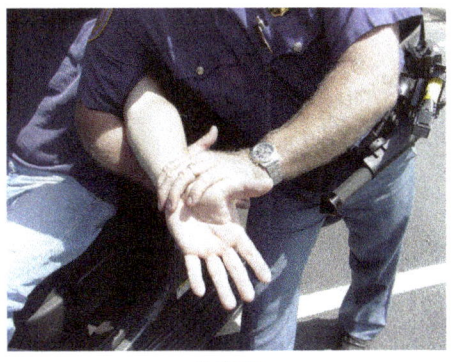

**10E**        **11E**        **12E**

Figures 10E, 11E, and 12E. Place your arm over the top of the suspect's upper arm as you reach under the suspect's arm, with your palm down. Keep pressure on the suspect's wrist with your left hand to stabilize his arm so the palm and forearm remain in the upward position.

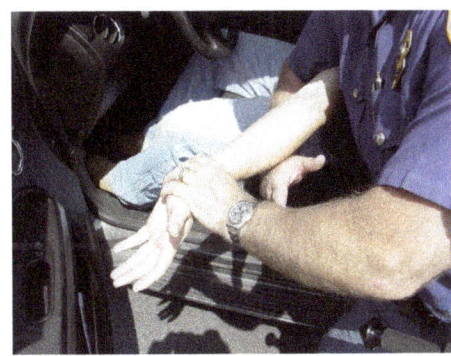  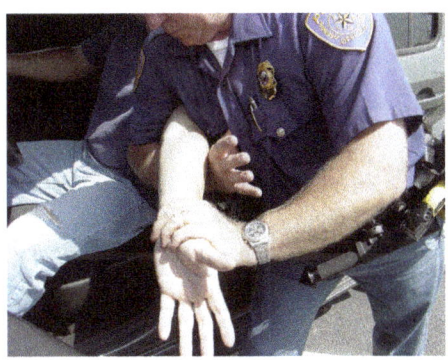

**13E**        **14E**        **15E**

Figure 13E. When your arm wraps around the suspect's arm, there is little room for movement. **This is a very powerful hold**.

Figure 14E. The officer's back remains straight, as he pushes forward slightly with his left hand, to assure the wrap around the suspect's arm will be tight, and allow a little distance between the suspect's arm and the officer's chest.

Figure 15E. Now that the suspects arm is wrapped, the officer reaches for his own lapel, with his palm toward his own chest.

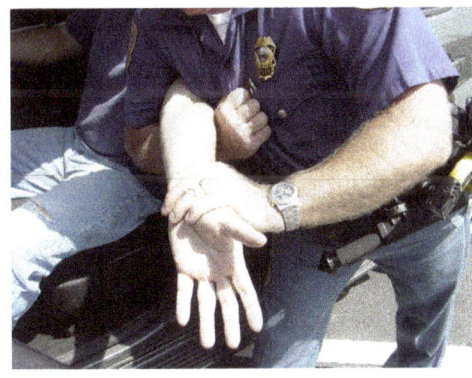

**16E**

Figure 16E. The officer reaches under the suspect's arm and grabs his own lapel in a firm grip. The height of the vehicle, relative to the officer, comes into play at this time. The officer may need to bend his right leg to come down to the suspect's arm. If the vehicle is taller than the officer, the suspect's arm will have to come down at an angle to accommodate the officer's height. The suspect's palm still remains in an upward position.

  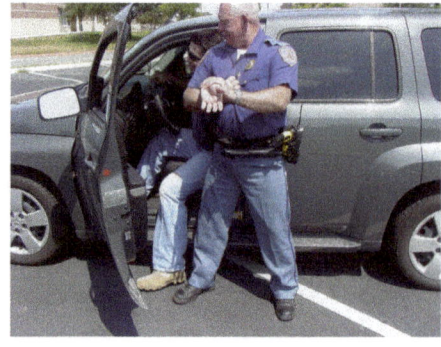

17E          18E          19E

Figure 17E. The officer tells the suspect to step out of the vehicle as he starts to stand erect. Commands are very important at this stage, due to the pressure being put on the suspect's arm. The suspect is feeling pain but does not know how to ease it, and may stay there waiting for you to tell him what you want done.

Figure 18E. When the suspect starts to exit the vehicle, straighten your back to increase the tension on the arm, not allowing the hold to loosen while centering your balance.

Figure 19E. Notice the position of the driver's feet as he exits the vehicle, and notice that the feet of the officer are planted in a fixed position. There is a slight turn of the officer's torso back to the left, allowing the suspect to get his feet and body out of the vehicle.

## CAUTION:

**This is the point of the extraction that needs to be slow and deliberate. Standing up too fast, not giving the suspect time to exit the vehicle as you turn, or turning too fast may injure the suspect.**

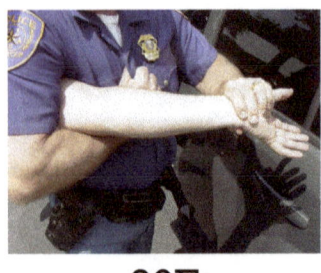   

20E          21E          22E          23E

Figure 20E. During the exit and while you're turning, the suspect's arm remains secured by a firm grip on your lapel.

Figures 21E, 22E, and 23E. Only your right leg moves, as you turn back to your left, allowing you to stay close to the vehicle you are turning the suspect into. The officer's back is straight during the entire turn.

24E           25E           26E

Figure 24E. When the suspect is close to coming up against the vehicle, turn his palm to face the vehicle. This will allow you to push the suspect's arm against the vehicle with your body for better control and more hyperextension if needed.

Figure 25E. Your right foot should move forward, as far as it can, just before the suspect comes in contact with the vehicle.

Figure 26E. After the suspect does make contact with the vehicle, your left leg now moves back to keep tension on the suspect's shoulder, keeping him up against the vehicle.

27E           28E           29E

Figure 27E. You will make sure that the suspect is up against the vehicle by over extending the suspect's arm. You have now turned 360 degrees from the start of this extraction.

Figures 28E. and 29E. The officer releases the suspect's arm from the figure four lapel lock. The left hand of the officer maintains his grip on the suspect's left arm with the suspect's palm toward the vehicle, and keeps the tension on the arm by pulling it back against his body. The officer still keeps pressure on the back of the suspect's arm during the release and gives himself room to get his arm out from the front of the suspect's arm. The officer's feet are still in the same position with the right leg forward and the left leg back.

30E

31E
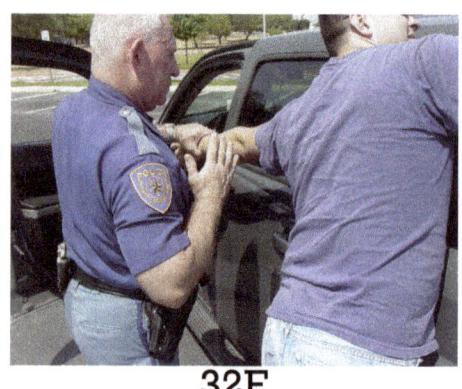
32E

Figure 30E, 31E, and 32E. When preparing to place the suspect's arm in the weakest position, your footing now changes with your left foot forward and your right foot back. Keep the suspect's left arm out to the side and under control, while pulling your right elbow back and bent below the suspect's elbow.

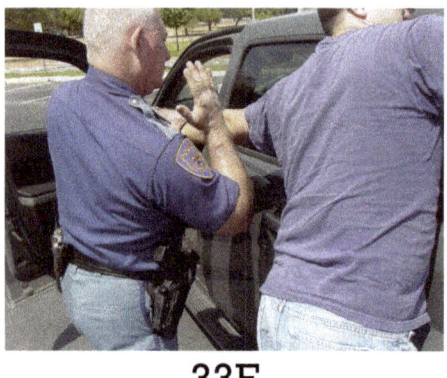
33E

34E
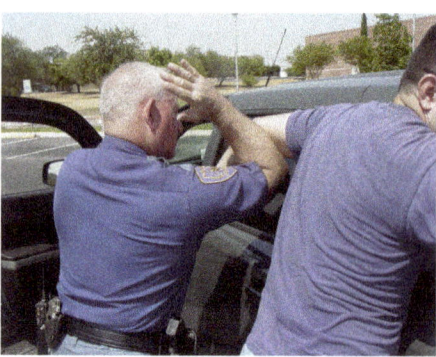
35E

Figure 33E, 34E, and 35E. Strike your right elbow upward, making contact with the suspect's arm just above his elbow. This strike will bend the elbow of the suspect upward. Assist the bending of the suspect's arm by guiding his arm inward to the weak position at the side of the suspect.

36E

Figure 36E. After the upward strike with your right elbow, bend the suspect's left arm inward to a downward position with your left hand. Start extending your right arm across the back of the suspect's arm. This forces the suspect's shoulder to roll forward.

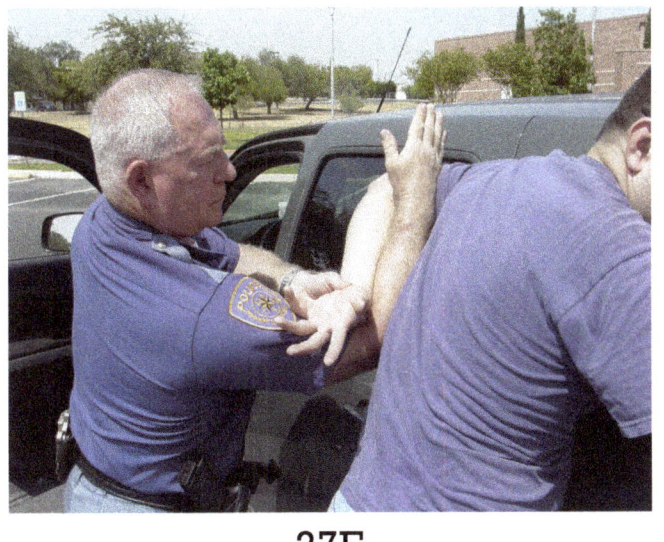 

37E  38E

Figure 37E. When you extend your left arm forward, your right hand will slide down the back of the suspect's arm until the heel of your right hand is at his elbow joint. The suspect's arm is placed across the top of your right arm, using your left hand.

Figure 38E. The officer can release his left hand grip after he has locked the suspect's arm with his right arm. This grip prevents the suspect from pushing downward with his left arm.

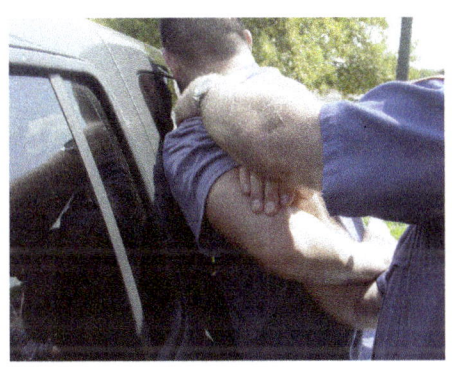 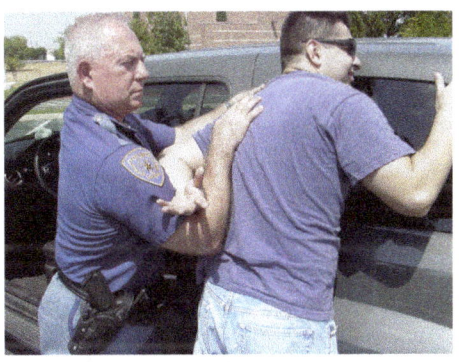 

39E  40E  41E

Figure 39E. Wrap your right hand over the back of the suspect's arm as you are bending your right elbow. This will secure the suspect's arm while reaching to the suspect's shoulder with your left hand in order to keep the suspect from turning.

Figure 40E. After the suspect's shoulder is secured with your left hand, move your right hand up on the suspect's back, turning your hand so the palm is down against the suspect's back. Press forward with your right hand while keeping the elbow bent and the suspect up against the vehicle.

Figure 41E. Now reach back for your handcuffs with your left hand.

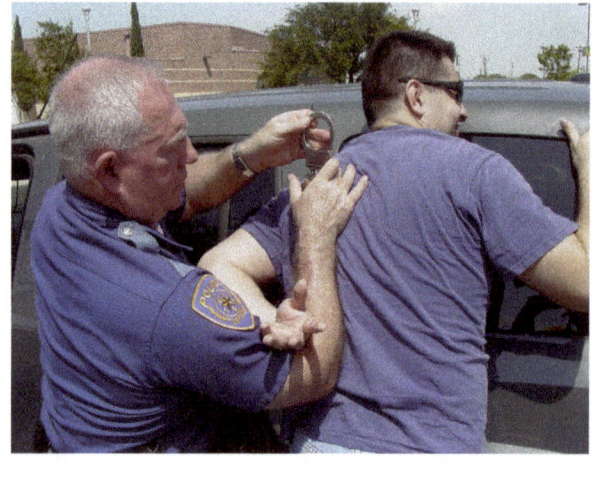
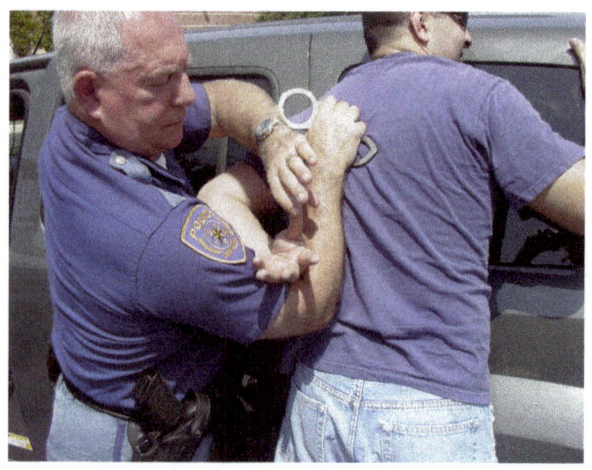

42E

43E

Figure **42E**. After removing your handcuffs with your left hand, they are transferred to the right hand which is still locking the left arm of the suspect.

Figure **43E**. After the exchange is made with the handcuffs, the left hand reaches down to the left hand of the suspect. The lock on the suspect's arm remains tight.

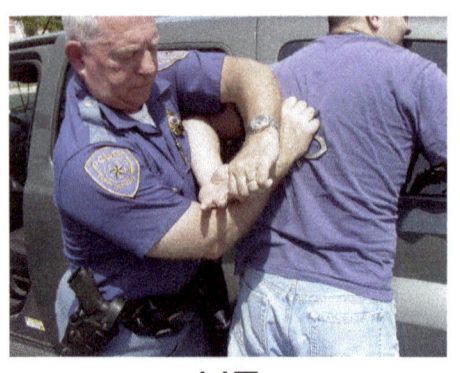
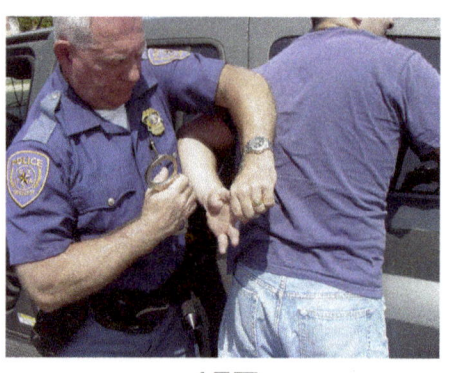
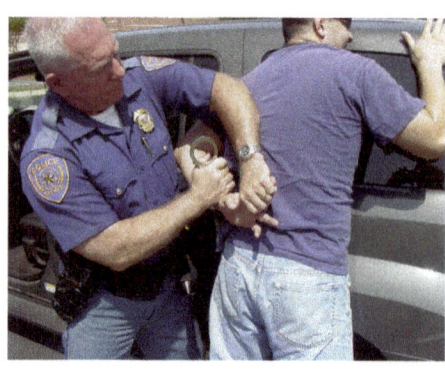

44E                                   45E                                   46E

Figure **44E**. Your left hand grips the index and middle finger of the suspect's left hand to gain control of both the hand and the arm. The right hand on the back of the suspect now pushes your elbow away from the suspect's back a few inches. This will allow your right arm to slip out easily and to keep the suspect's arm from being tight to his back.

Figure **45E**. After your right arm slips out from under the suspect's arm, with the handcuffs in your right hand, you want to make sure your grip on the fingers of the suspect is very tight. Keep suspect's arm a few inches away from his back to allow the handcuffs to be put on smoothly .

Figure **46E**. Using the finger lock on the suspect keeps him from pulling downward and away. Putting on the lower portion of the cuff first will make it easier when placing the other hand into the cuff.

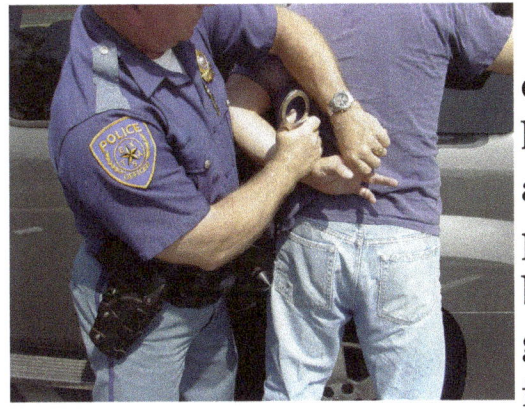

Figure **47E**. When placing the lower portion of the cuff on the suspect's left wrist, allow some room behind the suspect's wrist to allow the cuff to spin around and lock. When control is taken on the suspect's left hand, turn his fingers sideways not just back. Some people have great flexibility when the fingers are pulled back, but the best control is when the fingers are turned to the back and side.

47E

48E

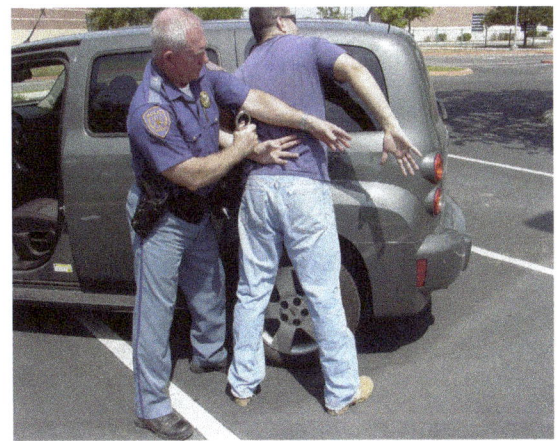

49E

Figure **48E and 49E**. The officer is standing to the front of the suspect's leg with his left leg to secure the suspect. The officer then asks for the suspect's other hand, in order to gain control of the suspect's hand before cuffing.

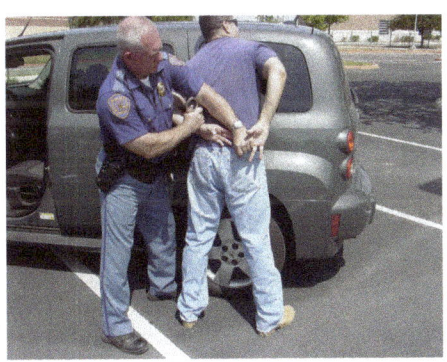

50E

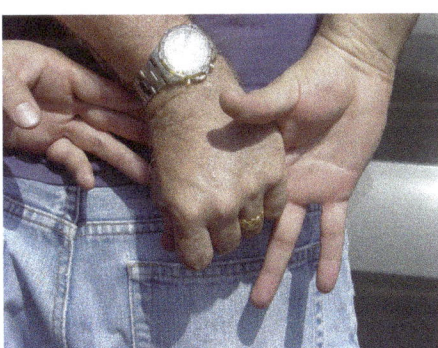

51E

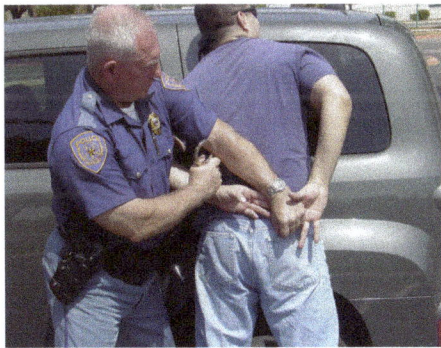

52E

Figure **50E, 51E, and 52E**. The grip on the suspect's right hand is again a finger lock, which is gained by reaching across with the left hand of the officer. The officer's hand is now turned with the thumb down and with the palm of his hand toward the suspect's back. The index and middle fingers are gripped as close to the suspect's hand as possible.

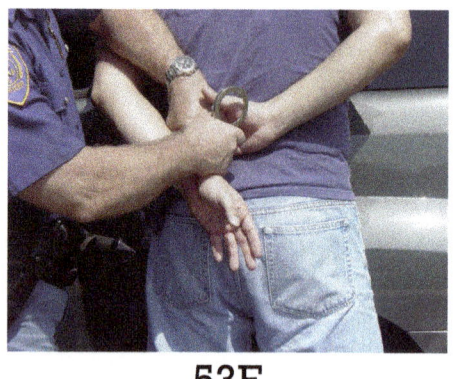 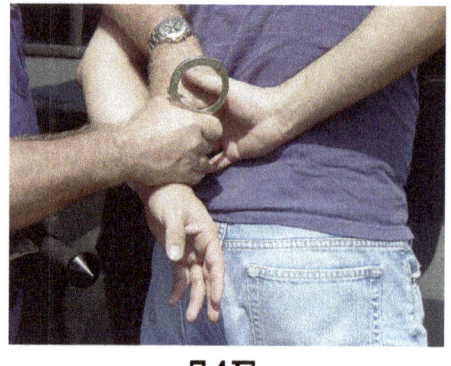 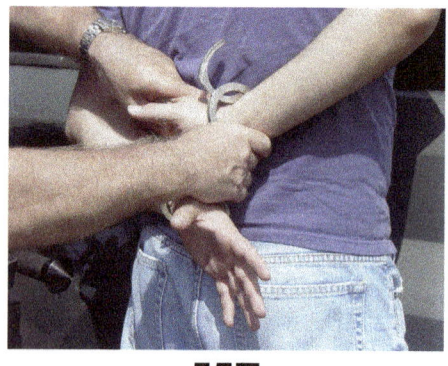

53E  54E  55E

Figure 53E, 54E, and 55E. Bring the suspect's arm across his back using the finger lock. The suspect's hand is brought far enough so the top end of the handcuff is at the suspect's wrist. Pull the suspect's hand slightly away from his back allowing room for the cuff to go around the wrist and lock.

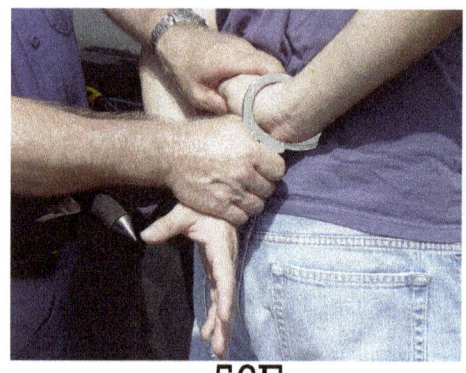 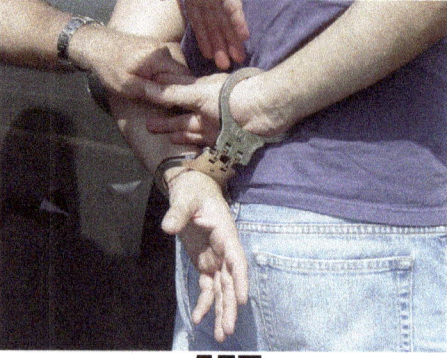 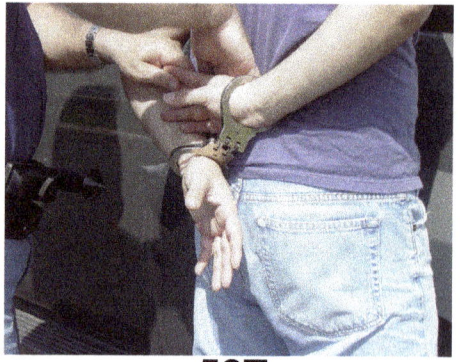

56E  57E  58E

Figure 56E. For great control when placing the handcuffs on a prisoner, the officer in this case has hinge cuffs, but the control over the cuff is in the center. Remember that this control is only for placing the cuffs on the prisoner and not moving the prisoner after being cuffed.

Figure 57E. and 58E. To move the suspect from this location, pull the hands of the suspect slightly away from his back. Your right hand will reach between the suspect's back and the cuffs. The back of your hand will be up against the suspect's back. Reach through toward the left hand.

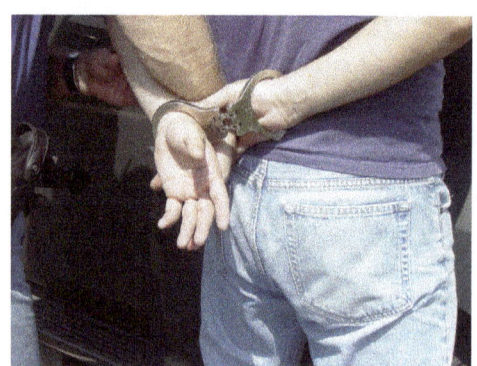

Figure 59E. Reach down between the suspect's back and the suspect's cuffed hands to his left hand. Use your right hand to do this. Prepare to grab the ring finger and the little finger together close to the suspect's left hand.

59E

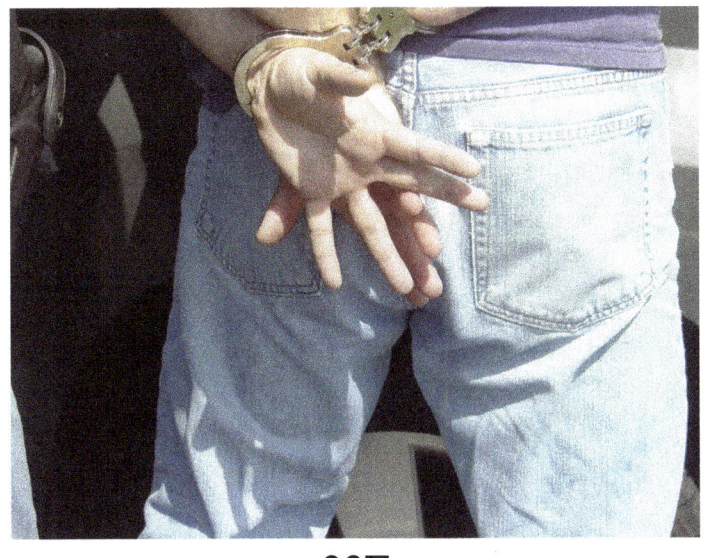
60E

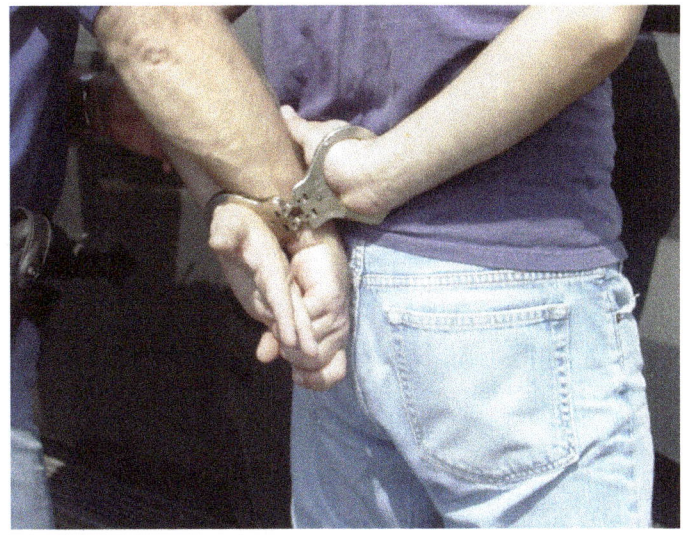
61E

Figure 60E. Reach through with your right hand and grip the little finger and ring finger together. Your palm is toward you, and the back of your hand is against the suspect.

Figure 61E. Grip the fingers as close as you can to the base of the fingers for the best control and to prevent injury to the suspect's fingers.

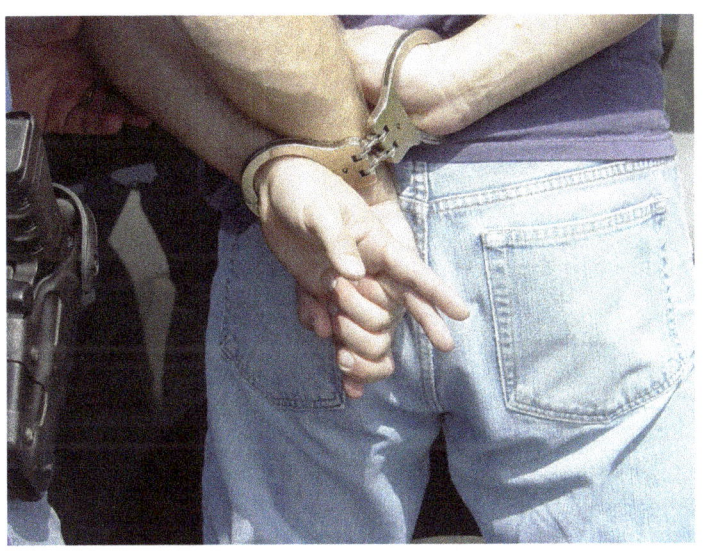
62E

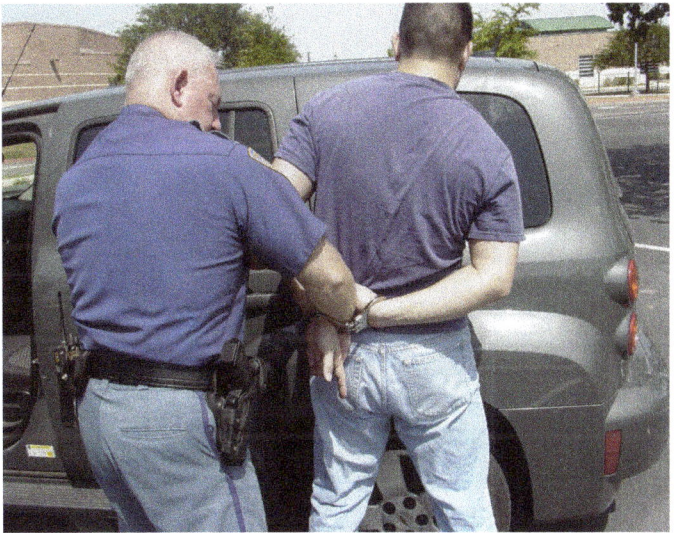
63E

Figure 62E, and 63E. Grip the suspect's fingers close to the base of his fingers for the best control over the suspect's hand. This will apply the maximum amount of tension when lifting the suspect's hand back up through the cuffs. Here is where you need to adjust the amount of tension needed to get the suspect to comply. **Fast movements should be avoided at this stage to prevent injury.** You have the suspect handcuffed. <u>**Take your time**</u>.

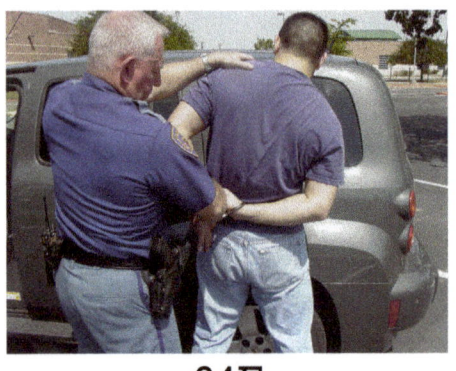  

64E  65E  66E

Figure 64E, 65E, and 66E. These figures show the officer applying pressure to the suspect's fingers by pulling the suspect's fingers up through the handcuffs. The handcuffs assist in locking the suspect's wrist when the fingers are lifted in an upward position. The suspect is now easily controlled and can now be moved.

# Control To Takedown Then Handcuff

# Figure Four Lapel Grab Exit

1F  2F  3F

Figure 1F, and 2F. The officer has the suspect's arm locked, as in Figure 40E in the figure four lapel grab exit. Moving the suspect without handcuffing is only slightly different. The officer's right arm is under the suspect's left arm so the suspect is not able to push his arm downward. The left hand of the officer reaches across the back of the suspect. Grip the upper back along the side of the neck for control. The officer stands close to the suspect with his left leg just to the left of the suspect for the officer's balance.

Figure 3F. When moving the suspect, pull down with your left hand to start his body bending to the side. This will off balance the suspect and guide him in the direction you lead his head. Your left foot moves back slightly for room to move the suspect to the left.

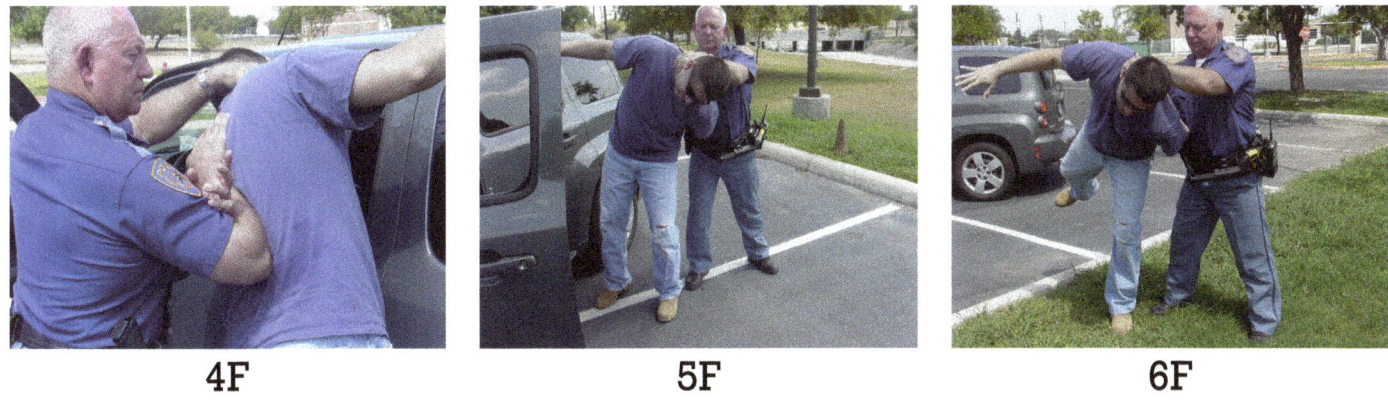

4F  5F  6F

Figure 4F. When the officer starts pulling down with his left hand, he keeps close to the suspect's back and bends his right arm. This will assure that the left arm of the suspect will not slip out of the locked position.

Figure 5F. When the suspect turns to his left, the officer's left foot steps back about 180 degrees, in order to take the suspect into a circular motion for the best control. Being off balance, the suspect will not be able to regain his balance and put up resistance.

Figure 6F. When you are ready to take the suspect to the ground, a little more pressure is applied with your left hand. Pressure is also applied to the suspect's back which lowers his left shoulder.

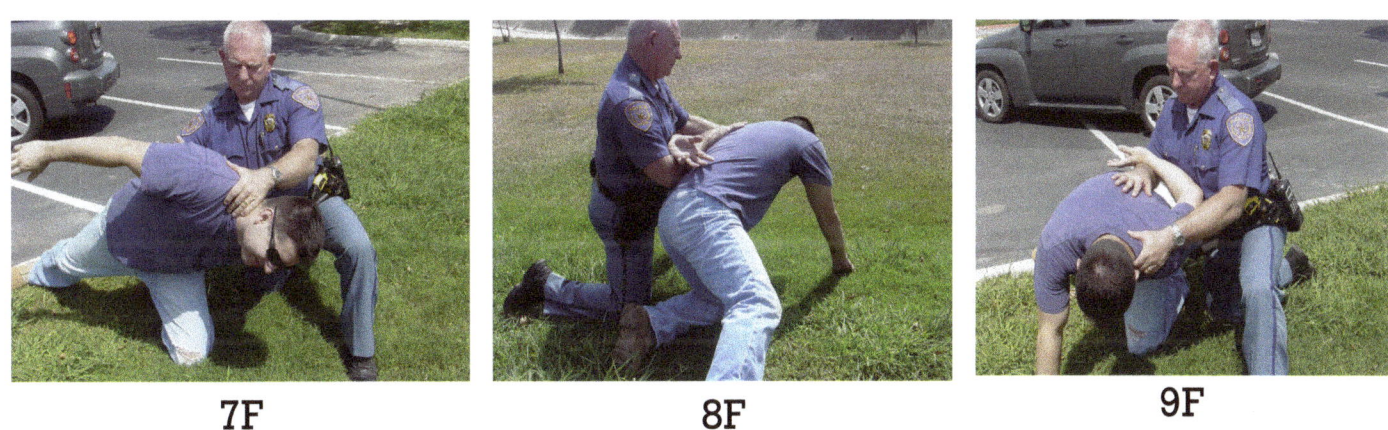

7F  8F  9F

Figure 7F. Assist the suspect to the ground by allowing him to put his left knee down. You control the speed of the suspect going to the ground by lowering your balance, kneeling alongside the suspect, and pulling back with your left hand.

Figure 8F, and 9F. Move your left hand to the suspect's left shoulder once he places his hand in front of himself for support. Your control is still maintained by keeping your right hand in place, locking the suspect's arm behind him.

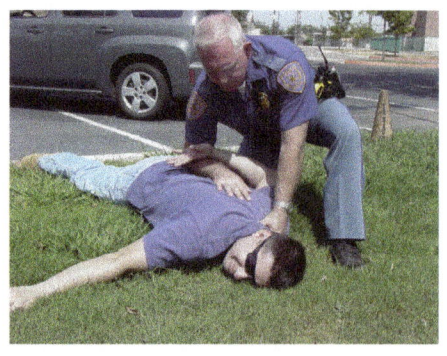 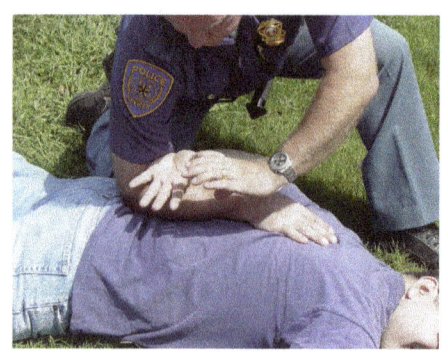 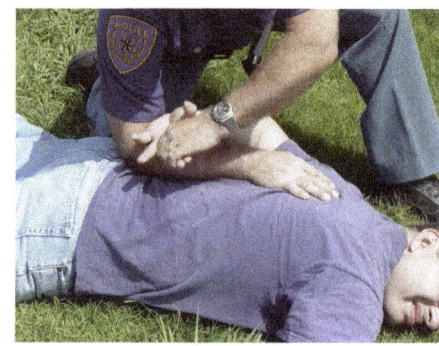

10F          11F          12F

Figure 10F. Place the suspect face down, and allow your right hand to keep pressure on the suspect's back. Make sure that his face does not hit the ground. When the suspect is lying flat on the ground, instruct him to place his right hand out to the side.

Figure 11F, and 12F. To overlap control, reach back with your left hand and grip the fingers of his left hand. The grip should be to the base of the fingers as close to the hand as you can get it. Grip the index finger and the middle fingers together.

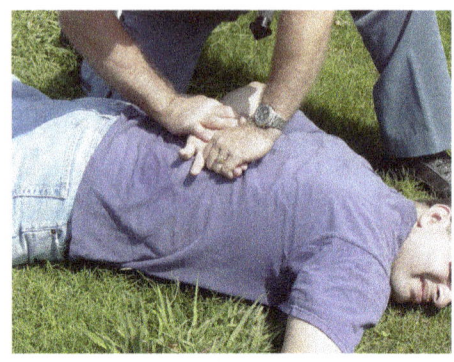 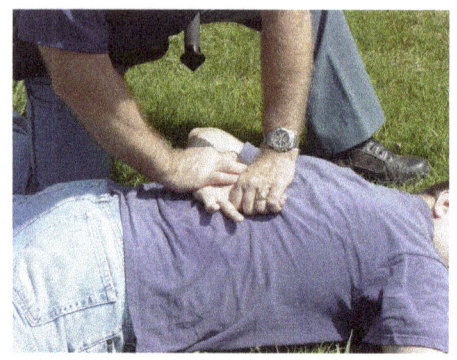 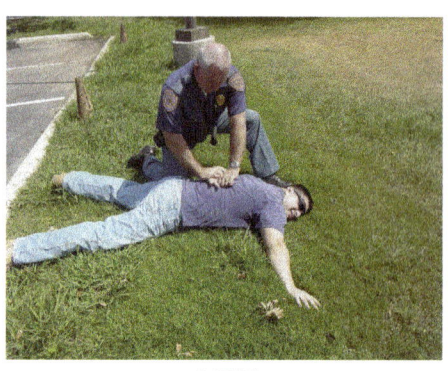

13F          14F          15F

Figure 13F, 14F, and 15F. After the finger lock is secure, you can move your right arm from under the suspect's arm. For maximum control, keep his left hand on his back, supported at the wrist with your right hand. This will keep his hand flat and not allow him to bend his wrist backwards. Pressure is placed on the suspect's hand with your right hand, and your left hand is able to maintain complete control by using the finger lock. By turning the suspect's fingers sideways, you create the most pressure for maximum control over the suspect, and prepare him to be handcuffed.

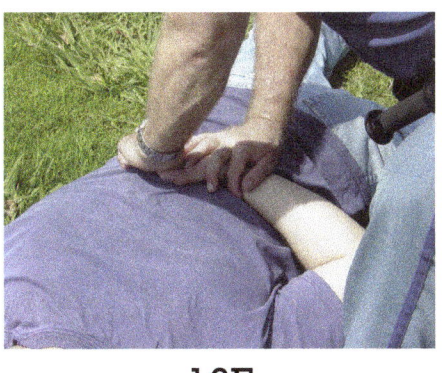
16F

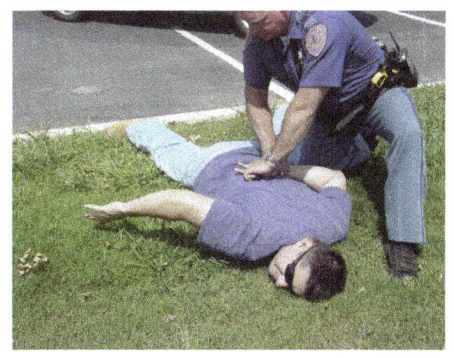
17F

Figure 16F. When the suspect is first taken to the ground, his hand is positioned on his back with his palm up. The officer keeps the suspect's hand flat by applying pressure to his wrist as he gets a grip on the suspect's fingers.

Figure 17F. When the finger lock is applied correctly, you will see a physical response from the suspect. The responses to look for are: the suspect turning his feet, bringing up his heels, or as in 17F, raising the arm that is loose.

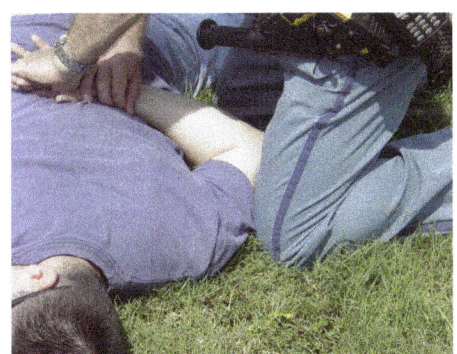
18F

19F

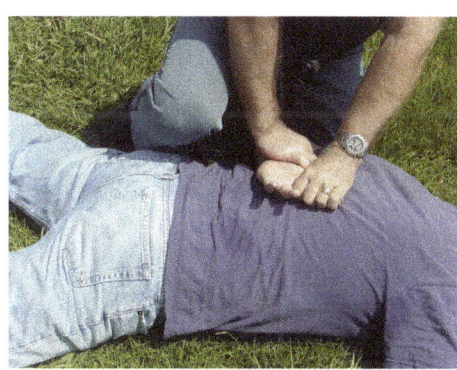
20F

Figure 18F, and 19F. After the takedown and finger lock, you will now prepare the suspect for handcuffing by kneeling your left knee behind the suspect's elbow while it is bent across his back. The knee prevents the suspect from moving his elbow back.

Figure 20F, and 21F. Your right knee will be brought up and placed behind the suspect's forearm, preventing the arm from moving down across his back.

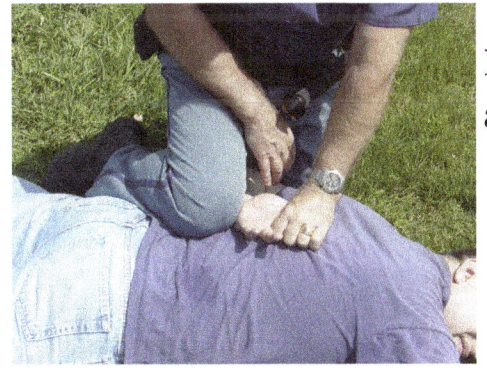
21F

Figure 20 F. Now the suspect's arm is secure from all angles, and you are free to handcuff.

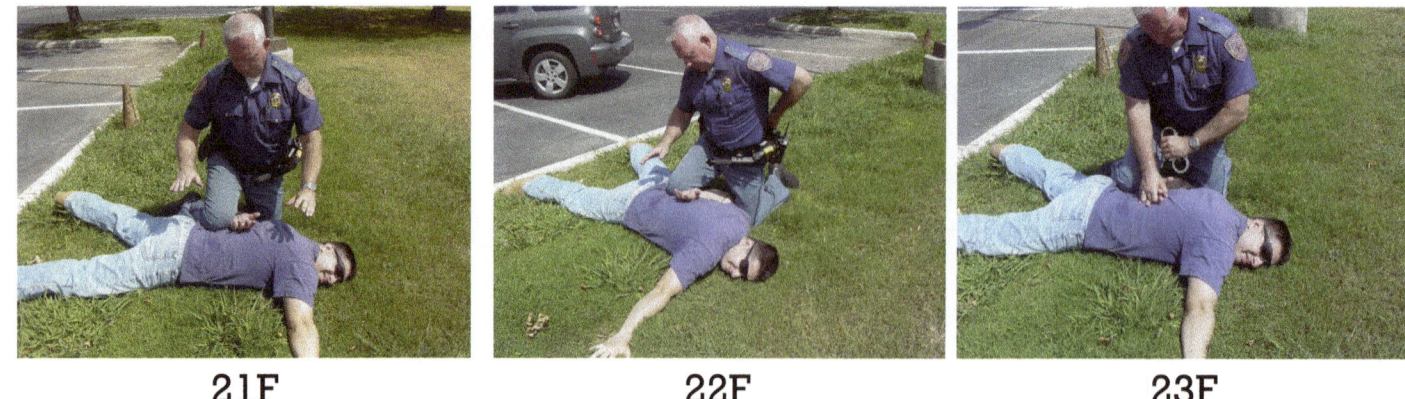

21F  22F  23F

Figure 21F. When the suspect's arm is locked in all directions with your knees, you are able to let go with both hands, allowing you to use your radio or reach for your handcuffs with either hand.

Figure 22F. The officer is reaching behind him for his handcuffs.

Figure 23F. When handcuffing the suspect, the officer positions his cuffs with his hand in the center for the most control over the cuffs. He reaches down with his right hand to gain control of the suspect's hand.

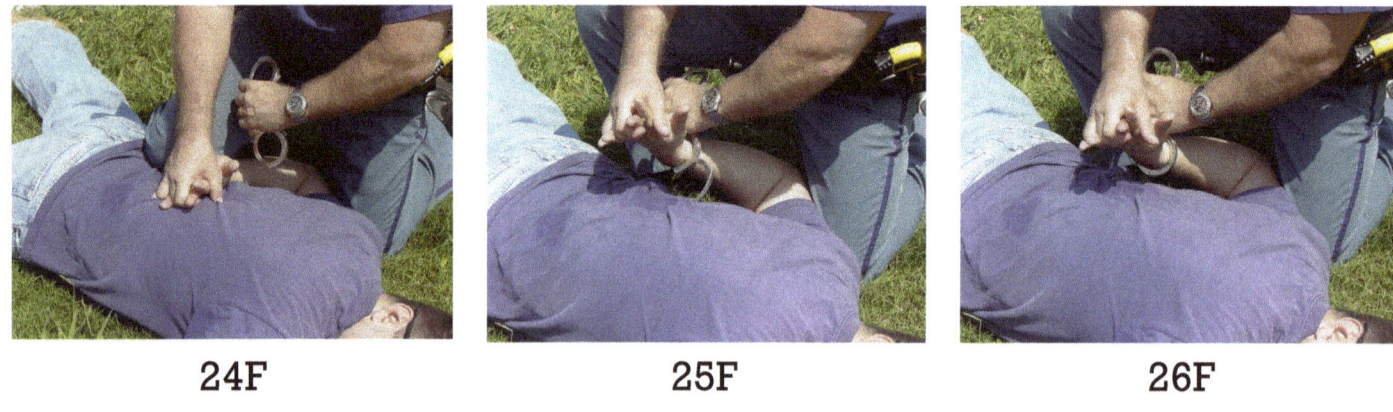

24F  25F  26F

Figure 24F. Grip the suspect's hand so that your fingers interlock with his, and you will have better control of his hand.

Figure 25F. Removing your right knee from behind the suspect's forearm will allow more mobility of the suspect's arm when you lift it away from his back. The arm is pulled upward off his back to make enough room for the cuffs to pass around his wrist without snagging his clothes.

Figure 26F. Secure the cuffs around the suspect's wrist.

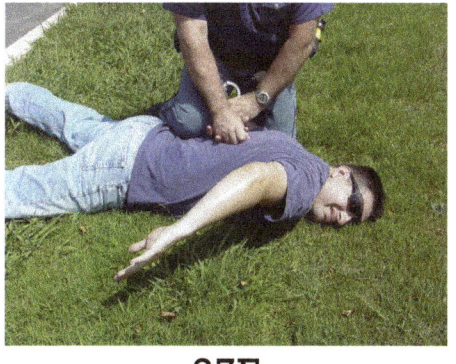 27F
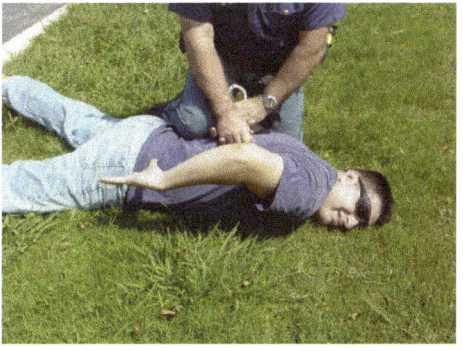 28F
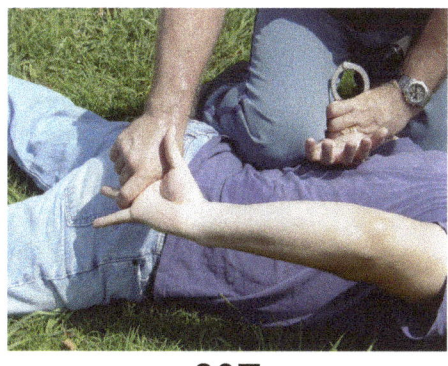 29F

Figure 27F. After the first cuff is in place, reapply the right knee to the suspect's back below his forearm to again secure the arm.

Figure 28F. While still in control over the suspect's hand, tell him to give you his other hand.

Figure 29F. Reach for the suspect's hand when it is close. Do not overreach, and lose your balance forward. Keep your weight back over your hips, and grip his hand so you are able to get a finger lock.

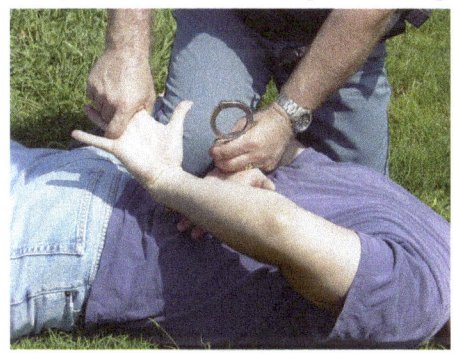 30F
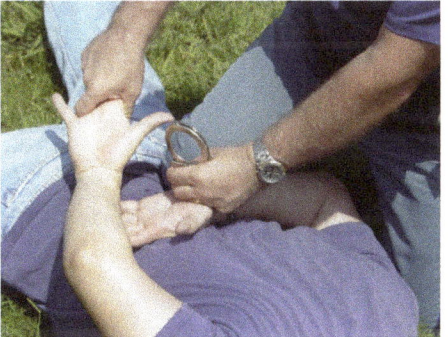 31F
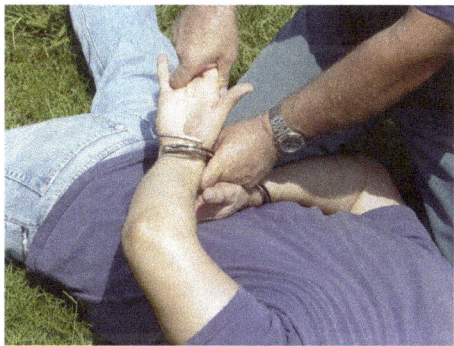 32F

Figures 30F, 31F, and 32F. Bring the suspect's arm across his back to meet the cuff, over the top of his hand. The cuff will have room to swing around the suspect's wrist and lock.

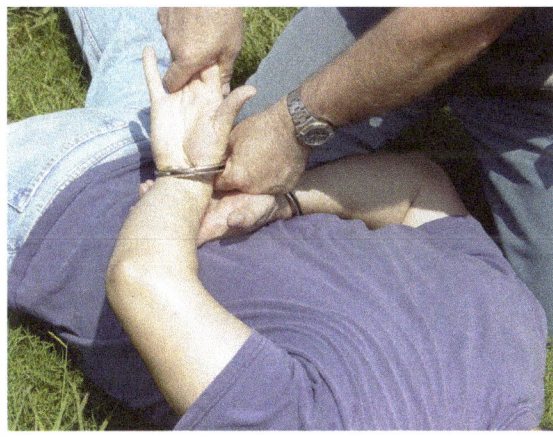

Figures 33F, and 34F. Lock the cuff around the suspect's wrist and make sure it is secure and tight enough.

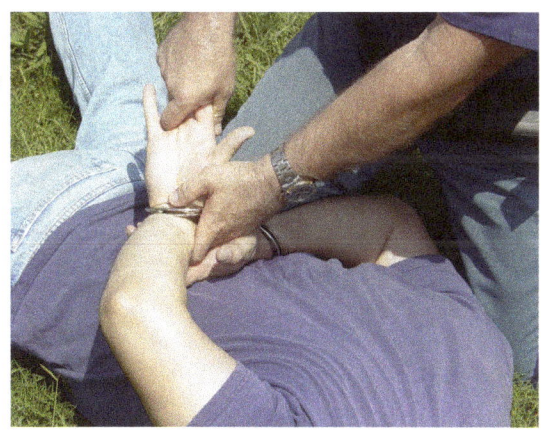

33F

34F

# Standing Your Prisoner Technique 1

After the suspect is handcuffed, **Technique 1** is a good way to stand your prisoner up without having to lift and pull him. This will prevent you from injuring yourself and make the transition of standing the prisoner much easier on both you and the prisoner.

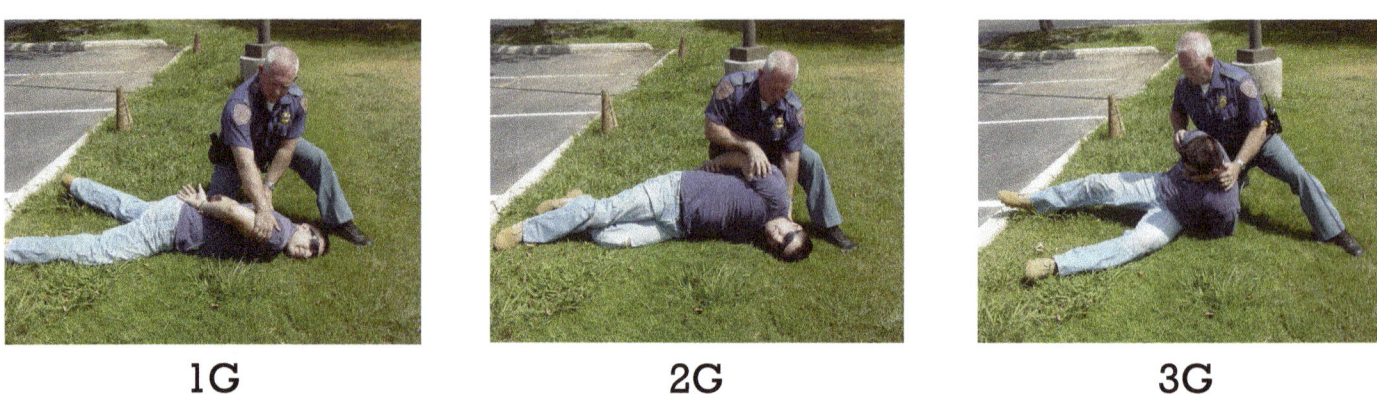

1G        2G        3G

Figures 1G, 2G, and 3G. Start this technique by telling the prisoner that you are going to roll him over to a sitting position. Put your left leg forward for support, and reach with your right hand across to the prisoner's right shoulder. Pull back with your right hand as you pull up and push forward with your left.

4G        5G        6G

Figure 4G. Set the prisoner upright, keeping him from leaning back with your left hand on his shoulder area. Allow your right hand to be free. Kneel on both knees to keep your balance.

Figure 5G, and 6G. Reach through between the cuffs and the prisoner's back with your right hand. Grip the ring finger and little finger of the prisoner so your thumb is against the prisoner's back. The fingers are lifted back up through the cuffs on the prisoner's side , putting pressure on the fingers and wrist with this lock.

7G            8G            9G

Figure 7G. The grip on the little finger and ring finger will apply the pressure as the prisoner's hand turns while you pull upward. His wrist will lock against the handcuffs. Caution is needed here to avoid injuring your prisoner while overlapping control.

Figure 8G. Press your right shoulder against the prisoner's back, and move your face to the left side, so he can not hit you with the back of his head. Maintaining pressure on his shoulder with your left hand also helps with your control.

Figure 9G. Instruct the prisoner to bend his knees so both feet are flat on the ground and lean back against you. You have now moved your right knee up behind the prisoner for balance.

10G            11G            12G

Figure 10G, and 11G. Instruct the prisoner now to push back against you and stand up. At the same time, you are pushing against the prisoner's back. Your left hand now moves to the upper left arm of the prisoner. The equal force against each other will allow the prisoner and the officer to stand smoothly without any lifting.

Figure 12g. Stand your prisoner upright making sure his feet are under him so he can safely stand on his own without any support from you. You still keep the finger lock with your right hand for control, and your left hand on the prisoner's upper arm. He is now ready to be taken to your vehicle or paddy wagon.

# Chapter 3
# Lapel Elbow Hyperextension

# Vehicle Extraction III
# Lapel Elbow Hyperextension

1H          2H          3H

Figure 1H. Approach the suspect's vehicle, blade your body so your weapon side is away from the door. Make sure the door is unlocked, and ask the suspect to step out of his vehicle. Take hold of the door handle to assist the door in opening.

Figure 2H, and 3H. After the door is open, instruct the suspect to extend his left hand out to the side. Reach with your left hand, palm down to grip the suspect's wrist to control the suspect's arm.

4H          5H          6H

Figure 4H. Grip the suspect's arm with your left hand, palm down making sure that the suspect's arm is extended and not bent.

Figure 5H. Step in with your right foot. Keep the suspect's arm extended and your back straight. Start turning the suspect's palm upward.

Figure 6H. Extend the suspect's arm forward and reach under the suspect's arm with your right hand. If the suspect is in a low vehicle, you need to lower your center by bending at the knees and not at your waist. Your feet need to stay apart to maintain proper balance.

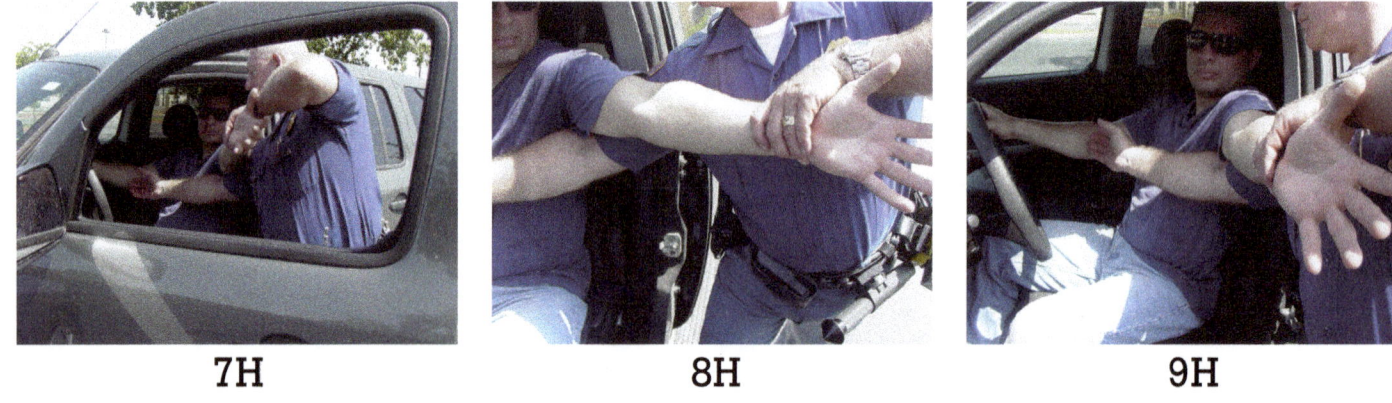

**7H**          **8H**          **9H**

Figure 7H, 8H, and 9H. While reaching under the suspect's arm, you need to continue to rotate his arm upward while keeping tension on the arm. Pull it forward to keep it extended. Your arm needs to be above the suspect's elbow close to the suspect's body as you reach forward.

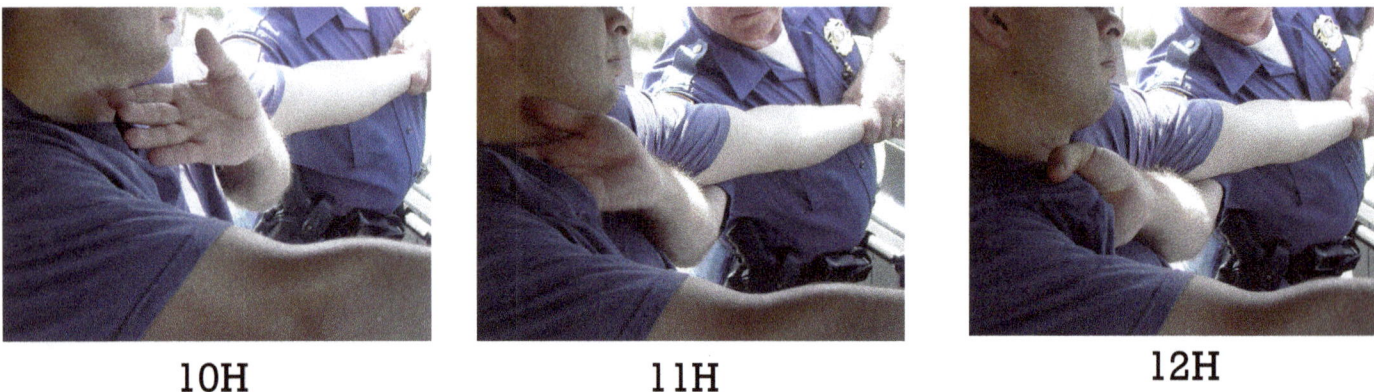

**10H**          **11H**          **12H**

Figure 10H. Position your palm forward as you reach under the chin of the suspect.

Figure 11H, and 12H. Reach inside the collar and grip along the right side of the suspect's neck. (*The heavier the material, the better your grip will hold. Jackets during the cooler months make this technique work the best.*)

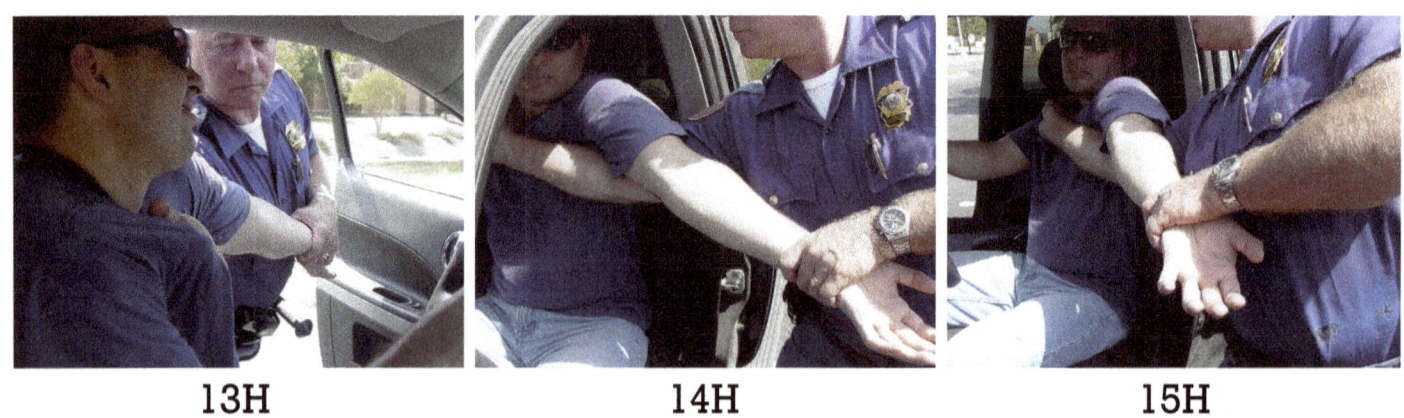

**13H**          **14H**          **15H**

Figures 13H, 14H, and 15H. After the grip is secure on the suspect's lapel, the grip on the suspect's left arm is now pressed downward to a lower level, using the officer's right arm as the fulcrum for the hyperextension of the suspect's left arm.

 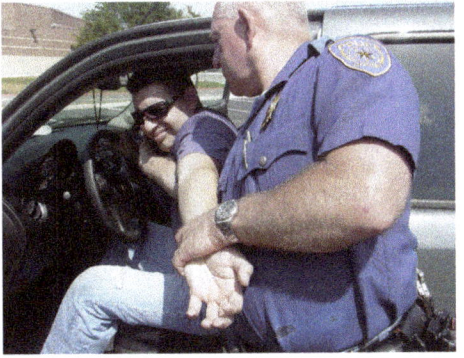 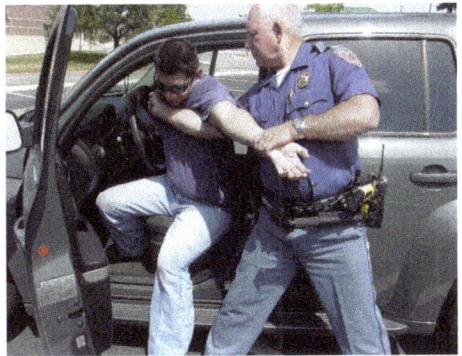

16H            17H            18H

Figure 16H, and 17H. Press downward with your left hand as you start turning back to your left side. The hyperextension on the suspect's arm will cause him to raise his shoulder, causing his center of balance to move to his head and neck. This transfer of balance allows the officer to lead the suspect out of the vehicle.

Figure 18H. To get the most leverage, the officer steps back with his left leg and places his back against the vehicle keeping his stance wide.

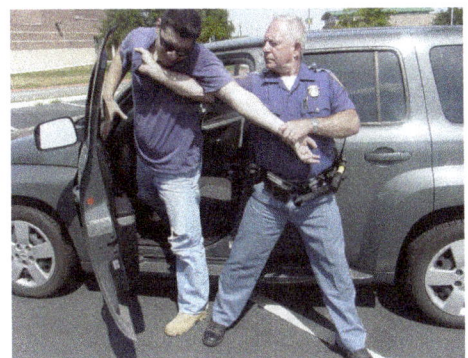  

19H            20H            21H

Figure 19H. Keep your stance wide until both of the suspect's legs are out of the vehicle. Your right arm is still fully extended to maintain the distance between you and the suspect. This will allow your left arm to be stable as the fulcrum of the suspect's arm is being pressed down on.

Figure 20H. When the suspect has both feet on the ground, turn back to the left, as you step forward to the left with your right foot. Stay just ahead of the suspect as he turns with you.

Figure 21H. As you continue turning to your left, the suspect will have to follow in a circular pattern. Again move your right foot forward, ahead of the suspect's feet as he turns. Continuing the movement keeps the suspect off balance as he turns toward the vehicle.

22H         23H         24H

Figures **22H, 23H, and 24H.** The tension is still on the suspect's left arm, as the suspect comes up tight against the vehicle. The left foot of the officer now steps back so he can continue applying tension .

25H         26H         27H

Figure **25H.** The tension on the suspect's lapel is taken off by raising your left hand allowing the hyperextension of his arm and shoulder to lessen.

Figure **26H.** You now remove your grip on the suspect's lapel, and pull your hand back.

Figure **27H.** When your arm is pulled out from under the suspect's left arm, it bends at the elbow, and you cock your right arm.

Figures **28H and 29H.** When the right arm is cocked, it comes back to allow room to get under the suspect's left elbow. Your right foot remains forward.

28H         29H

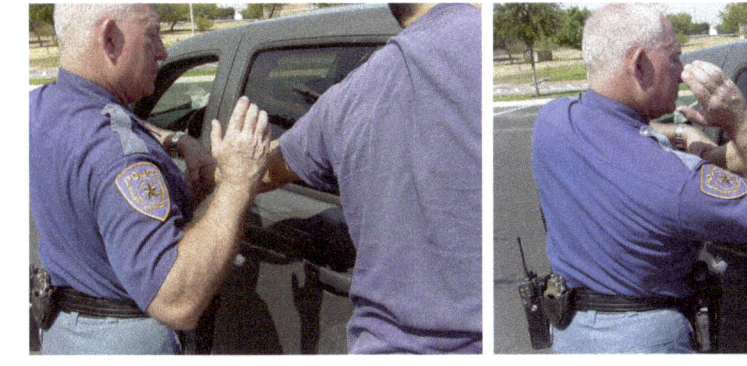 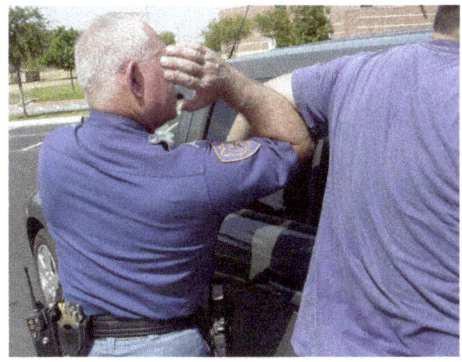

30H  31H  32H

Figure **30H**. The arm of the suspect should be turned palm toward you at this point. The suspect's arm will now bend upward and not be injured from being bent.

Figure **31H**. You bring your right elbow upward, striking above the elbow of the suspect. By using the bent forearm portion of the arm, this strike is not painful and does not cause injury to the suspect.

Figure **32H**. When the suspect's arm is struck, it will bend at the elbow. The officer's left hand assists in bending the suspect's arm toward his body so no force is necessary. The suspect's arm is now in the weakest anatomical position to cause resistance. This allows the officer to move the suspect's arm easily.

 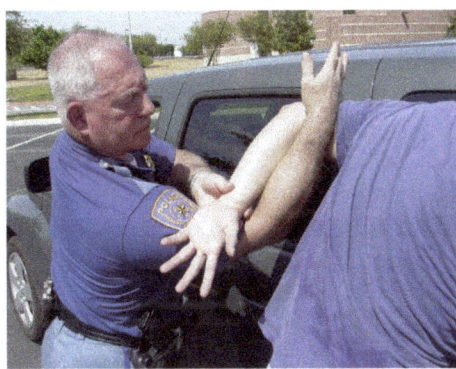 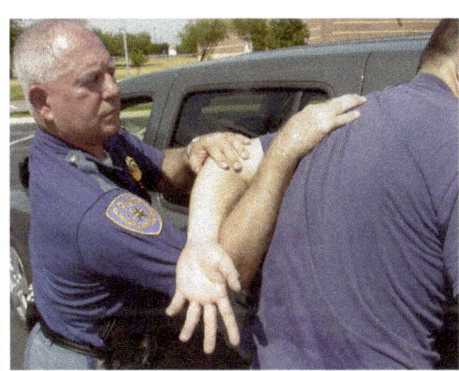

33H  34H  35H

Figure **33H**. After the suspect's arm is bent by the officer's elbow, he then extends his right arm. This rotates the suspect's shoulder forward while tilting his left hand back toward the officer.

Figure **34H**. The officer assists the suspect's left hand over the top of the officer's right arm, locking it in so it can not be extended.

Figure **35H**. When the suspect's hand has passed the officer's arm, the officer turns his right hand over onto the suspect's back, and bends his right elbow to lock the suspect's arm in. The left hand of the officer is placed on the suspect's elbow, pulling it downward to square the suspect's shoulder, and secure the lock.

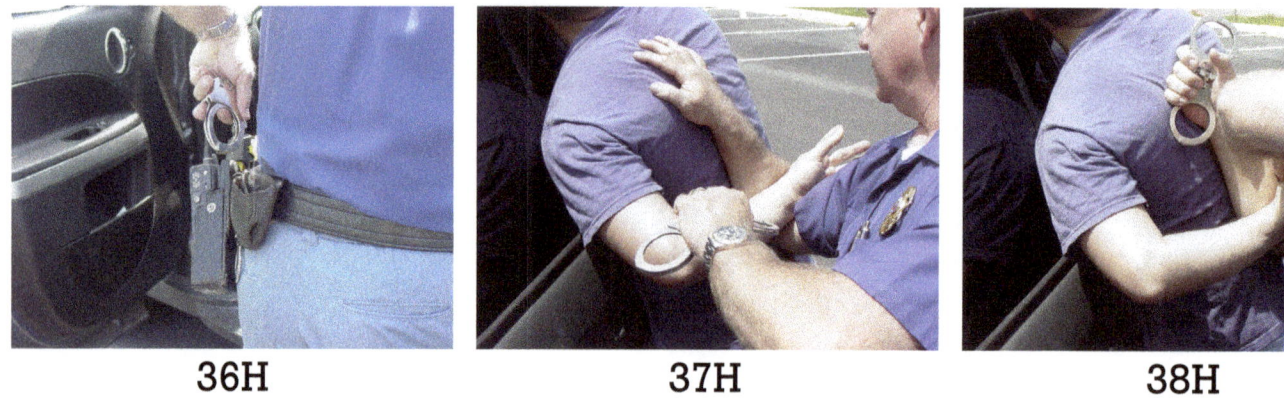

36H            37H            38H

Figure 36H. Reach back with your left hand, and draw your handcuffs.

Figure 37H. After removing your handcuffs with your left hand, they are transferred to the right hand, which is still locking the left arm of the suspect.

Figure 38H. After the exchange is made with the handcuffs from your left hand to your right hand, your left hand reaches down to the suspects left hand, and the index finger and the little finger are placed in a locking position. The lock on the suspect's arm remains tight with your right arm at this same time.

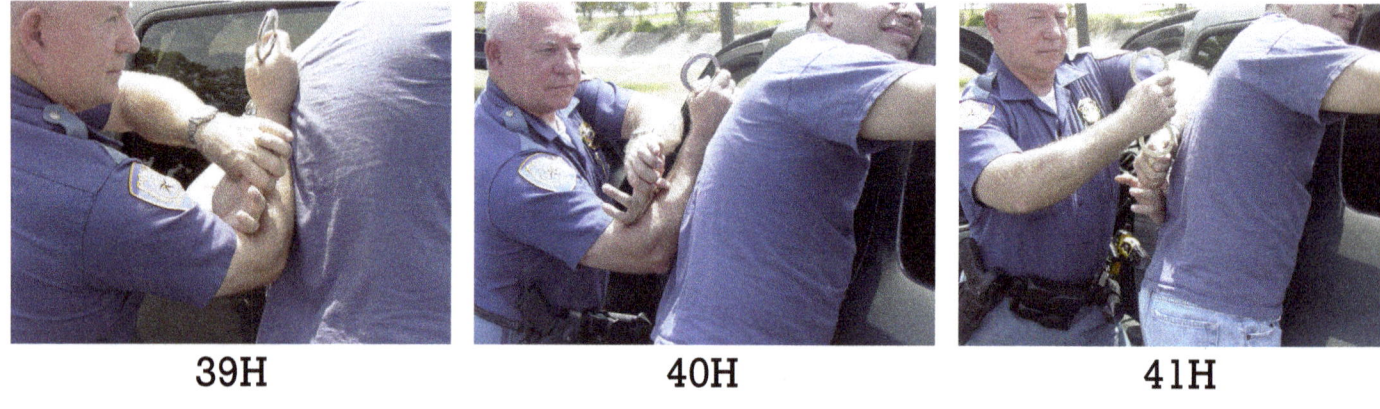

39H            40H            41H

Figure 39H. When grabbing the suspect's left hand for control, the palm of your left hand is facing his back. You will place your hand palm to palm on his, while grabbing two to three fingers. This depends on your hand size in comparison to the suspect's.

Figure 40H. When grabbing the fingers of the suspect, it is important to keep his hand in a flat position, and to grab deep into his hand. The grabbing deep means when your fingers grab his, you are **not** grabbing just the ends of his fingers, but as close to the hand as possible; as deep into the "web part" of hand.

Figure 41H. When the finger control is accomplished, slip your right arm out from under the suspect's left arm. This will leave the control with the finger lock and the pressure you apply with your left forearm against the suspect's left shoulder. The handcuffs are in your right hand and able to be moved in any direction to accomplish handcuffing.

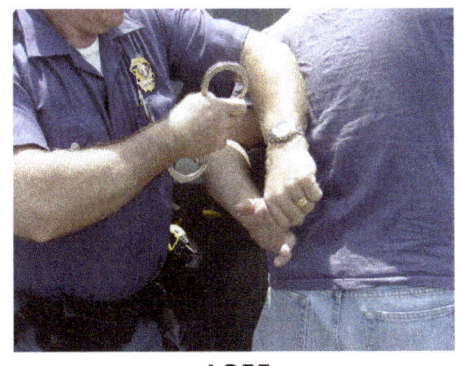 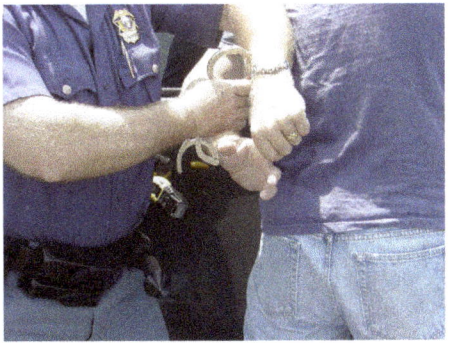 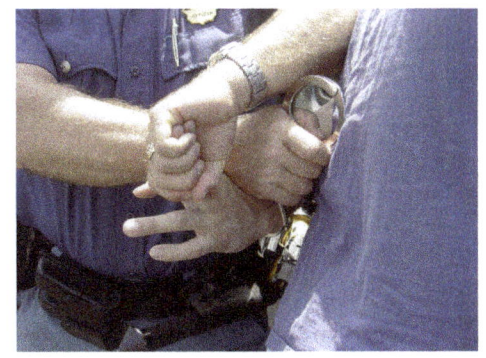

42H  43H  44H

Figure 42H. With the control on the suspect's hand, now move his hand back toward you away from his body. This space will allow you to place the handcuffs around his wrist.

Figures 43H, and 44H. Press the handcuffs on the suspect's wrist, while still controlling the suspect's hand, making sure your cuffs lock.

45H  46H  47H

Figures 45H, and 46H. Now with a handcuff on the suspect's left wrist, continue to hold the cuff in your right hand, keeping the suspect's left arm bent behind him. Direct the suspect to give you his right hand. Reach across the suspect's back with your left hand.

Figure 47h. Take another finger control lock with your left hand, on two or more fingers of the suspect's right hand, as his arm is brought back toward you.

48H    49H    50H

Figures 48H, and 49H. Take control of the suspect's hand, using a finger lock, and bring it back far enough to allow the cuffs to be placed on his right wrist.

Figure 50H. When placing his right hand in the cuff, bring his hand away from his body if possible, allowing you enough room for the cuff to close without snagging any clothing.

51H    52H    53H

Figures 51H, and 52H. After pressing the handcuff on the suspect's right wrist, you can see that the bottom of the cuff was placed on the left hand first so that there is no extra turning of the suspect's wrist necessary to complete the cuffing when the right hand is brought across.

Figure 53H. Make sure the cuff is secure , and to the tightness required so the suspect can not slip out of the cuff, but still allowing for circulation.

# Moving A Handcuffed Prisoner

One of the best techniques to move a handcuffed prisoner is by using another finger lock. This lock will allow you the most control with the least effort.

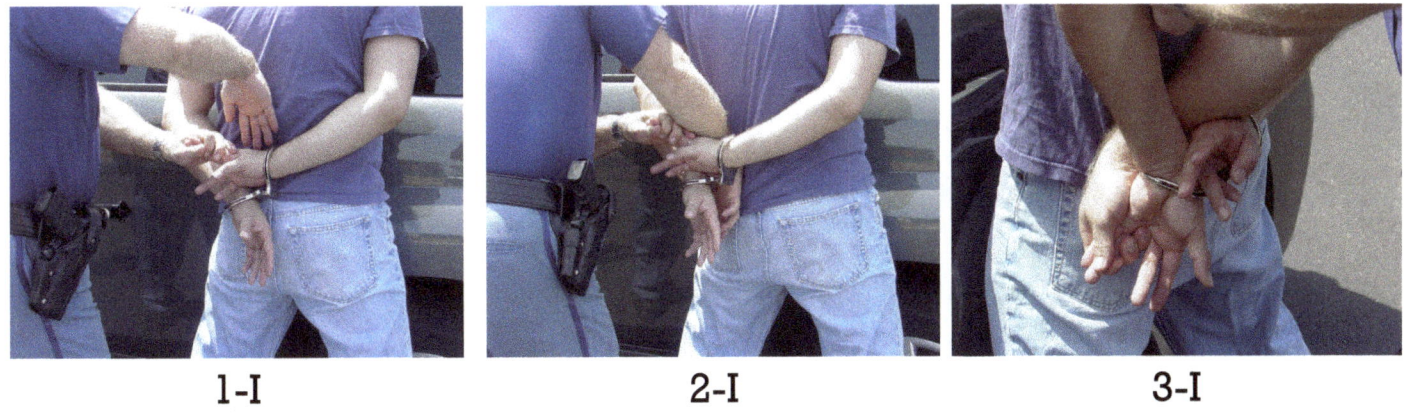

1-I  2-I  3-I

Figure 1-I. After the hands are handcuffed, to continue your control over your prisoner, use a finger lock. For the best control, use your right hand, with the palm toward you, placing it up against the back of the suspect, and reach behind the cuffs.

Figure 2-I, and 3-I. Reach down behind the prisoner's hands with your right hand. Grip his little finger and the ring finger together, close to his hand.

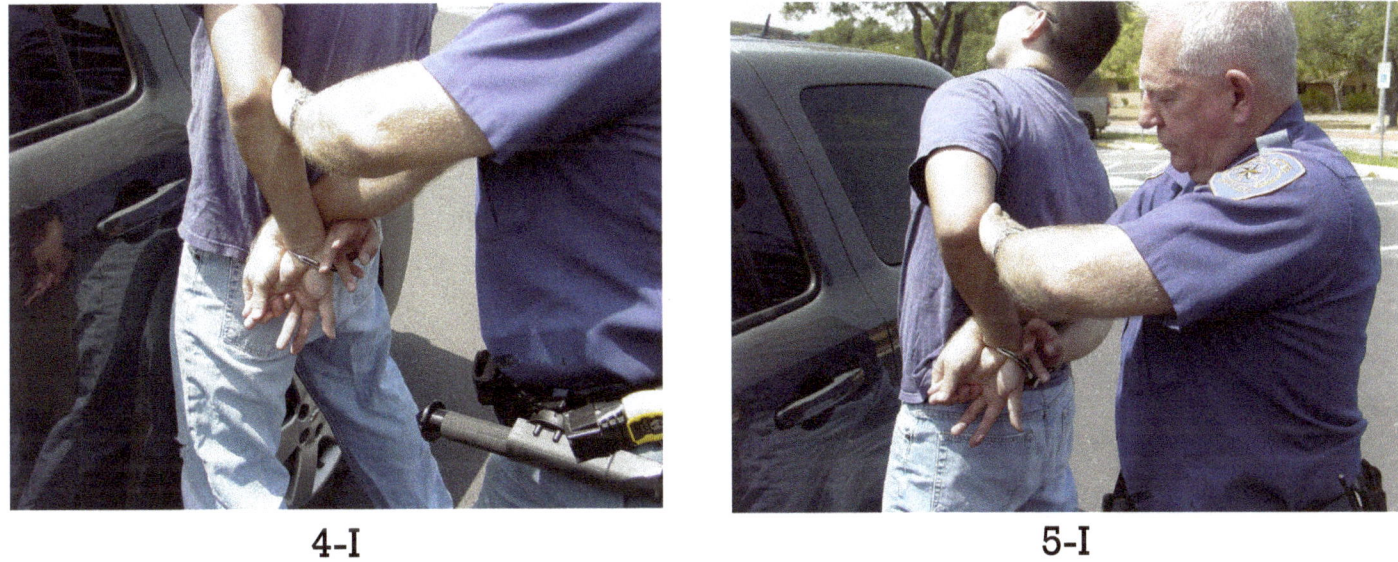

4-I  5-I

Figures 4-I. When your right hand has reached the side of the suspect's left hand, grasp his ring finger and the little finger together. At this point, the amount of pressure needed to keep complete control is minimal. When the fingers are lifted back up toward the cuffs, the amount of pressure you apply at this time depends on the amount of resistance the suspect will give you.

Figure 5-I. Apply pressure to the little finger and the ring finger with your right hand. Lift the fingers up and to the side for control in moving the suspect. Remember, the pressure on the fingers is sideways not back. Pulling the fingers back allows the hold to be less effective. Some people have a great amount of flexibility in their fingers and bending them back may not have an effect.

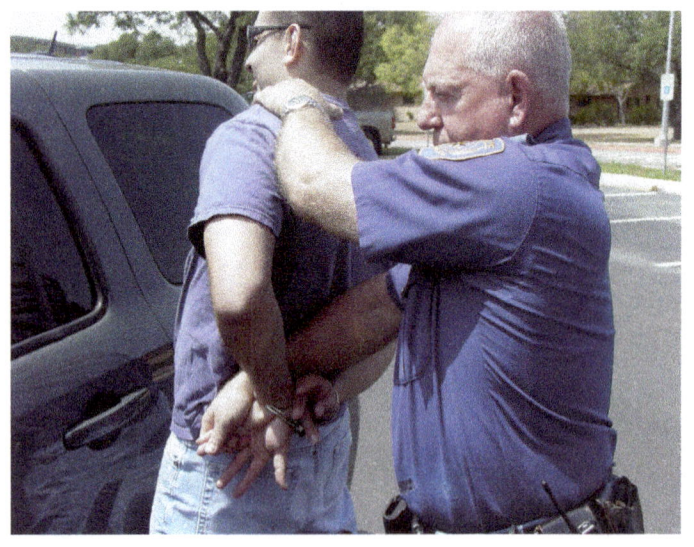 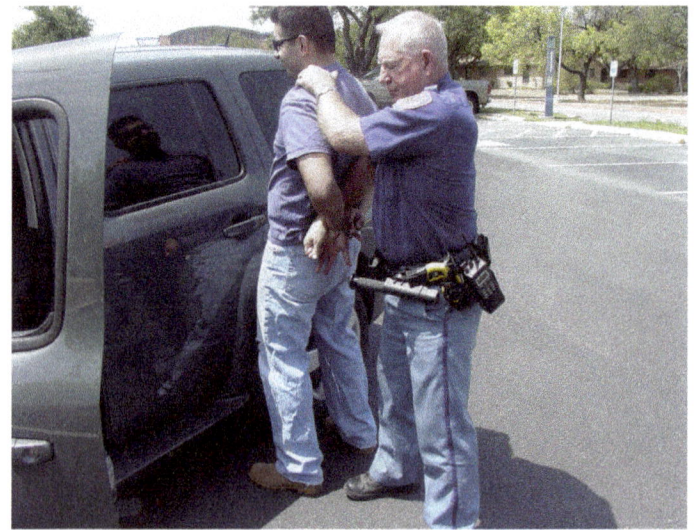

6-I                            7-I

Figure 6-I. After the fingers are gripped correctly, move your left hand to the suspect's left upper shoulder area. Placing your hand on the shoulder in this fashion, gives you better control, and prevents the suspect from throwing his head back into your face.

Figure 7-I. Now you are ready to move your suspect. The first movement should be with your left leg stepping out to the left side, as you turn your body and the suspect at the same time. Guide the suspect by using his left shoulder to steer him in the direction you want him to go.

# Chapter 4
# Baton Hyperextension

# Vehicle Extraction IV
# Baton Hyperextension Exit

1J          2J          3J

Figure 1J. After the approach, the officer opens the door and makes sure that the seat belt is removed and prepares to draw his baton. Drawing the baton will vary from officer to officer depending upon where he may carry it, and the type that is carried. This technique works with the expandable baton as well as the fixed.

Figure 2J and 3J When drawing the expandable baton in a cross draw, the baton is drawn to the strong side of the officer, where it is swung down to that side.

4J          5J          6J

Figure 4J. Extend your expandable baton quickly with a hand snap in order to lock it firmly, so it will not collapse when used.

Figure 5J. Bring your baton forward to your left hand. This will give you some support and stability on the front of your baton while changing your grip.

Figure 6J. Change your grip from a thumb down grip to a thumb up grip on your right hand. This grip will give you a stronger control over your baton, for the position that is needed in this extraction.

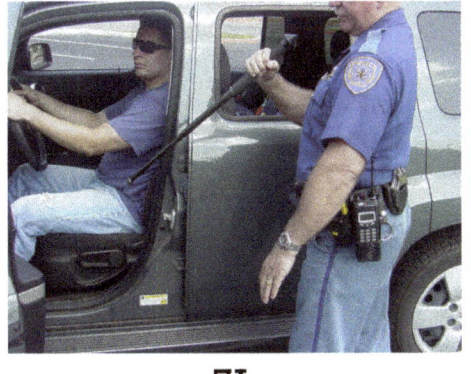  

7J        8J        9J

Figure 7J. When your grip is secure, bring the distal end forward and pointed toward the inside of the vehicle.

Figure 8J. As you bring the distal end of the baton up and into the driver's side of the vehicle, place it at the belt line of the driver. Tell the driver to stick his left hand out of the vehicle, at the same time, as you reach forward.

Figure 9J. Grasp over the top of the suspect's wrist, as it is extended from the side of the vehicle. The wrist and forearm should be kept forward and the arm straight.

 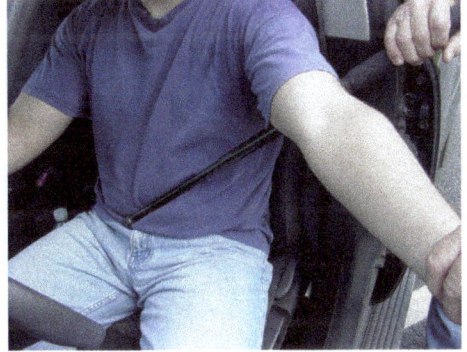 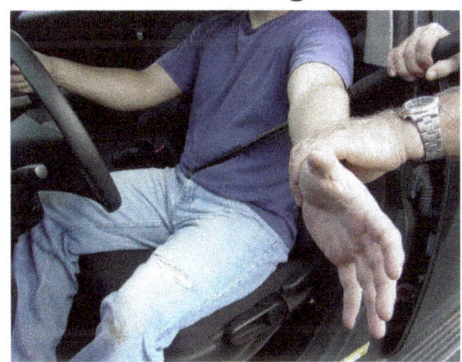

10J        11J        12J

Figures 10J, 11J, and 12J. Grip the wrist with your left hand, making sure the distal end of the baton is at his beltline and across the lower abdomen, about midline. Bring the other end of the baton up behind the triceps of the suspect's left upper arm. Keep the suspect's left arm extended.

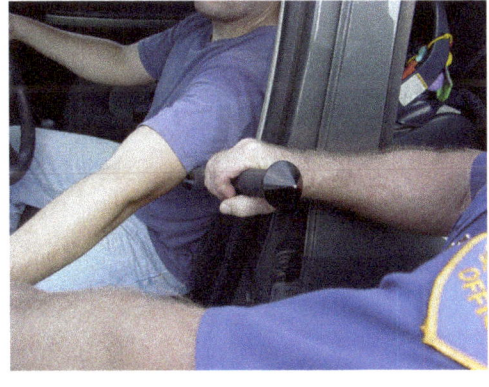

Figures 13J and 14J. Press forward with your right hand, causing the baton to tighten at the suspect's waist and apply pressure across the back of the suspect's arm. This will cause the suspect to move his left shoulder forward and lock his arm in place at the same time.

13J        14J

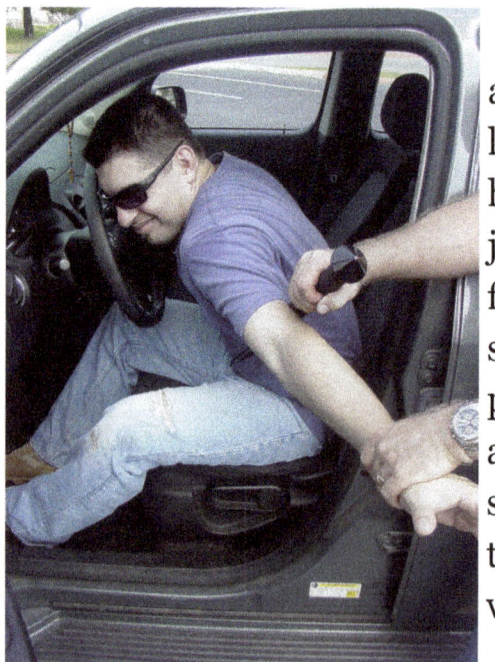

Figure 15J. When applying pressure with the baton across the back of the suspect's arm, do it slowly and a little at a time. This baton position across the back of his arm is very painful and if done quickly will cause injury. Use the amount of force necessary to bend him forward so his face is close to the steering wheel. At the same time you are pushing the baton forward, you are pulling back with your left hand at the suspect's wrist area. This position is creating a hyperextension of the suspect's arm. While all this is happening at the same time, you need to be telling the suspect to step out of his vehicle, as his body leans forward and to the left side.

15J

16J

17J

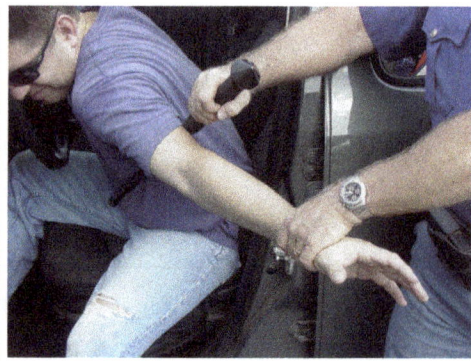

18J

Figure 16J. Observe that the arms of the officer are both straight, and his stance is at an angle with the right foot forward and the left foot back.

Figure 17J. As the suspect steps out of the vehicle, allow him time to get his feet on the ground, but not to be able to stand upright.

Figure 18J. The officer is still gripping the suspect's wrist, keeping the suspect's left arm forward and straight, not allowing the arm to bend.

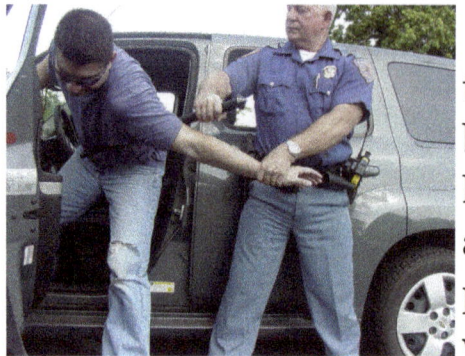

Figures 19J and 20J. Maintain the pressure across the back of his arm, as both of his feet get on the ground and you start turning the suspect to your left so that he will not hit the door.

19J

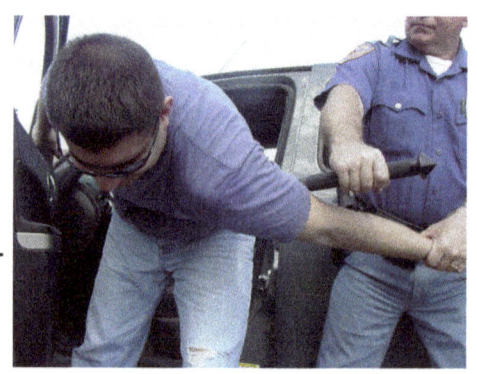

20J

64

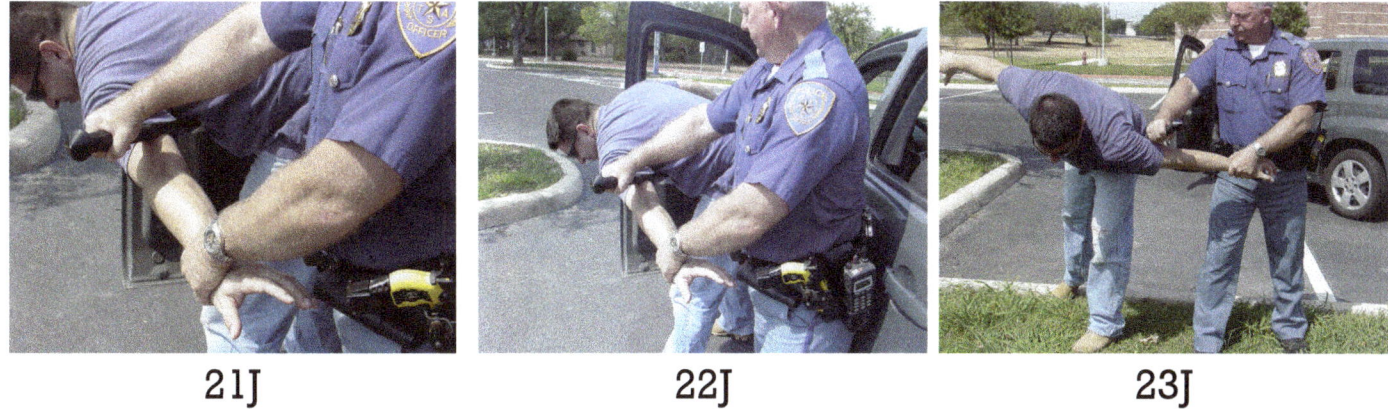

21J            22J            23J

Figure 21J, and 22J. Once the suspect has both feet on the ground, and the pressure is still on the back of his arm, the baton is locked in place at this time. The suspect is able to be moved in any direction forward by the officer.

Figure 23J. For the takedown, the officer just presses down with the right hand on the baton, and controls the suspect's speed, as he guides the suspect down. The officer will use his left hand on the suspect's wrist for the appropriate leverage.

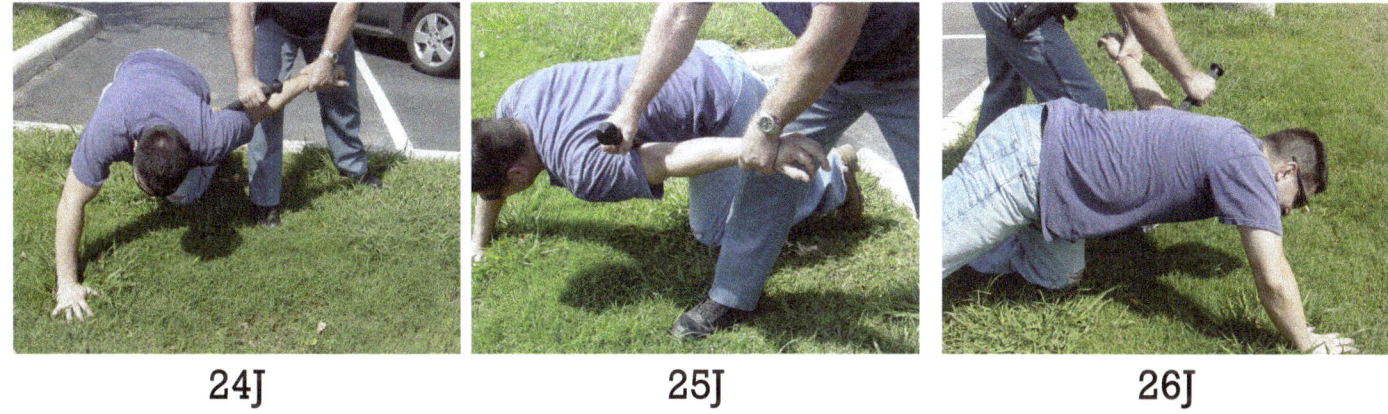

24J            25J            26J

Figures 24J, 25J, and 26J. Keep the angle of the baton across the suspect's abdomen and the back of his arm - allowing the suspect to put his hand down on the ground to stop himself from falling on his face. Keep the suspect's left arm out to the side, as you come down to the ground with him.

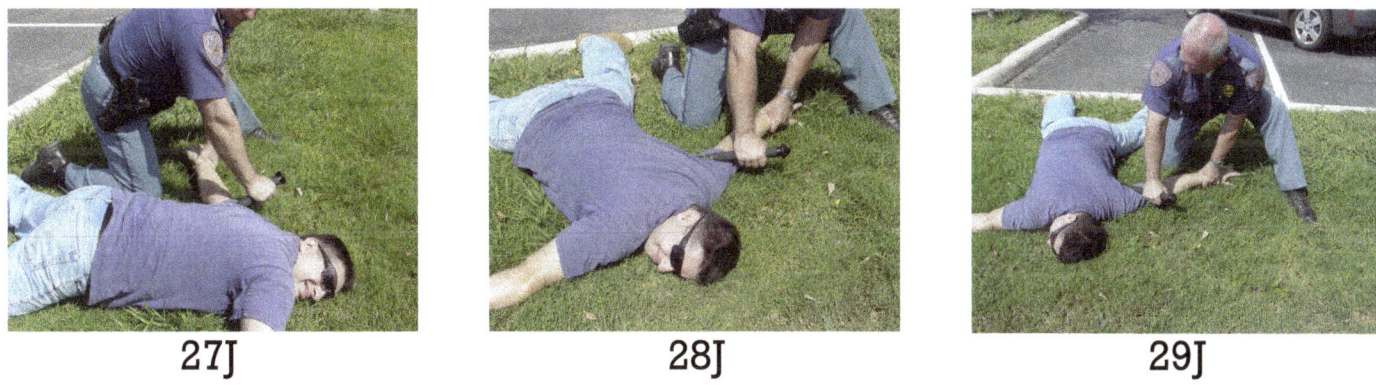

27J            28J            29J

Figures 27J, 28J, and 29J. After the suspect is on the ground, the officer kneels and continues to keep the pressure on the baton and the suspect's left arm out to the side.

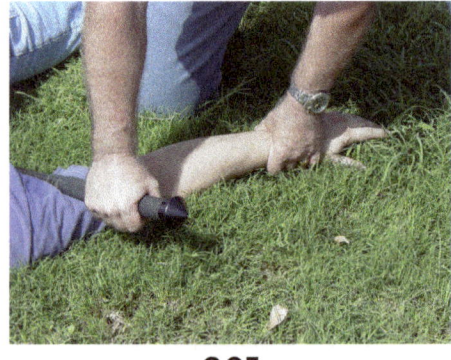 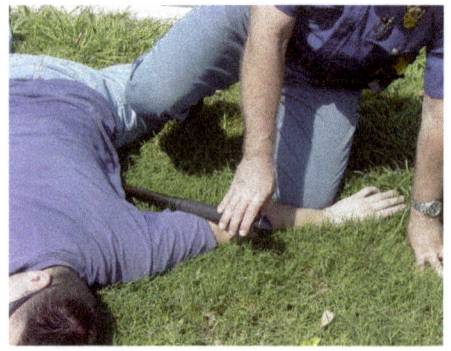 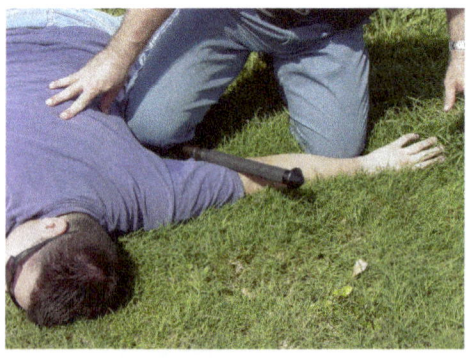

30J    31J    32J

Figure 30J. The direct pressure on the baton behind the suspect's arm will keep the suspect's shoulder down against the ground. The suspect's own body weight will keep the distal end of the baton in place under the suspect.

Figure 31J. The officer now moves his left knee behind the suspect's left arm so he will not be able to move it down toward his body. When the knee is in place, the left hand of the officer is able to be removed from the suspect's wrist.

Figure 32J, and 33J. The right knee of the officer is brought up and placed between the suspect's body and the baton, allowing the officer to take control without the use of his hands.

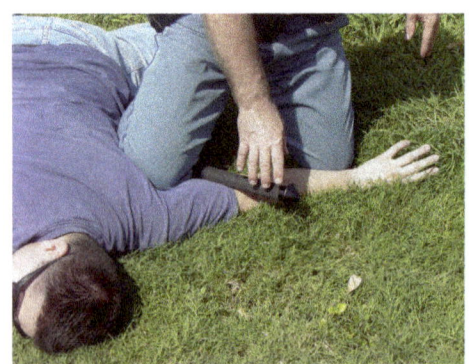 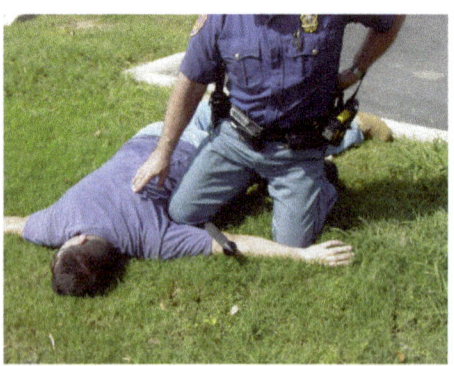 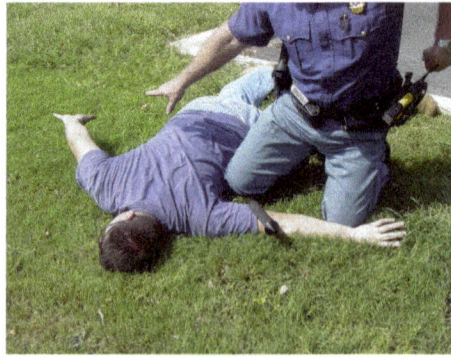

33J    34J    35J

Figure 34J. When the officer decides to handcuff the suspect, he now has both hands free to reach for his cuffs or use the radio if needed. Remember that the pressure you are applying on the back of the suspects arm is painful.

36J

Figure 36J, and 37J. Once the officer has his handcuffs in hand, he tells the suspect to bring his right arm back. The officer reaches for the hand but not enough to be off balance when reaching.

36J

66

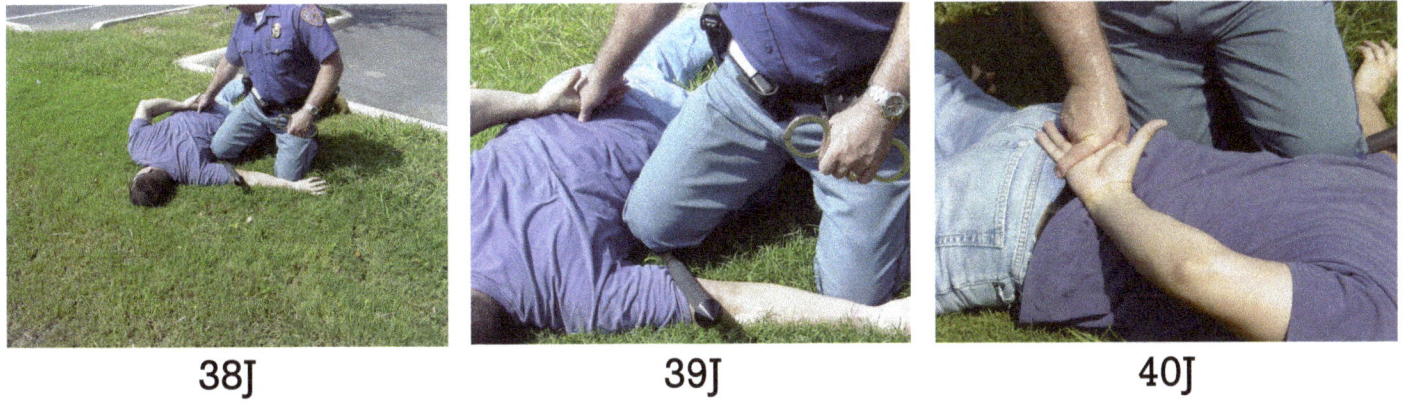

Figures 38J, 39J, and 40J. Grip the suspect's right index and middle finger with your right hand, as close as you can to the suspect's hand. Pull his hand as close as you can to the mid-back. Continue to keep pressure on the baton with your left knee.

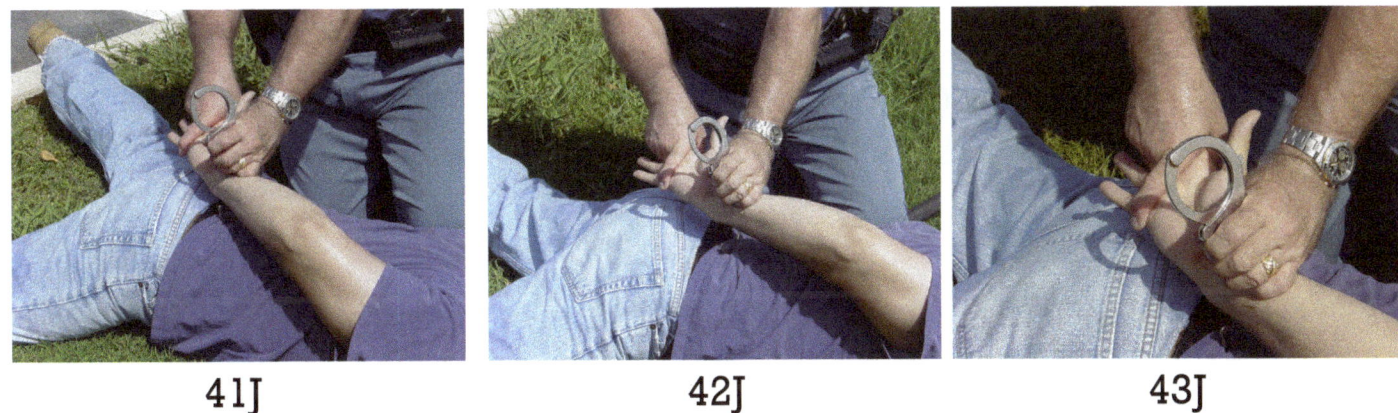

Figures 41J, 42J, and 43J. Placing the handcuffs on the suspect's wrist will require you to lift his arm up off his body, using your finger lock. Keep the suspect's hand as flat as possible, not allowing him to bend his wrist forward. Press the handcuffs on the suspect's wrist with your left hand. The space between the suspect's wrist and his body will allow the cuffs to close without snagging his cloths.

Figure 44J. Keep pressure on the finger lock until you are sure the cuff is secure around the suspect's wrist.

Figure 45J. Now let go of the finger lock with your right hand, and switch hands on the handcuffs, grabbing them in the middle for control.

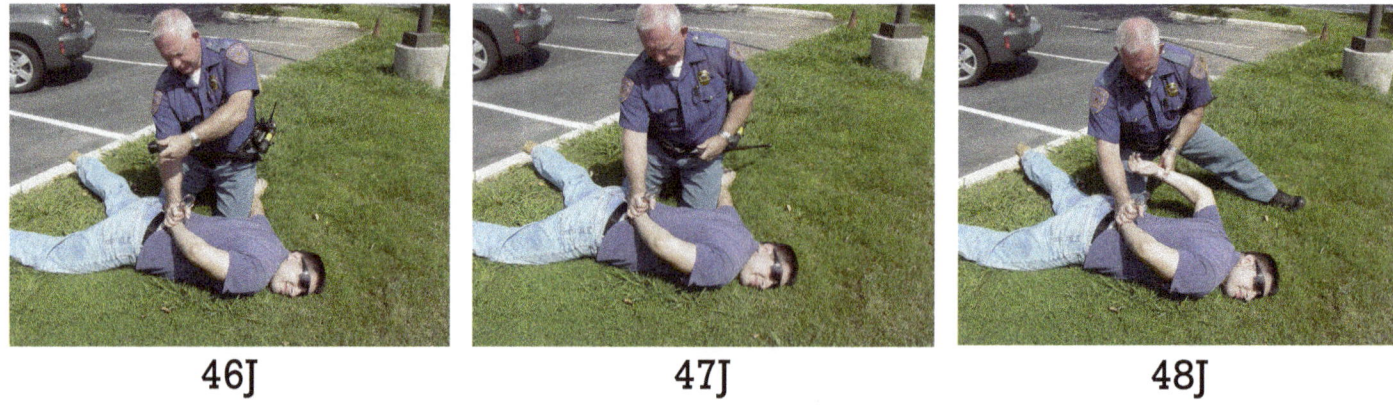

46J  47J  48J

Figures **46J, and 47J**. When the cuffs are secure on the suspect's right wrist, you can now remove the baton out from under the suspect. Place the baton back on your belt, in the holster if you can, or on the ground near you for your control. Keep the baton out of the reach of the suspect. Leave your knee behind the suspect's left arm.

Figure **48J**. After your baton is secure, raise your left knee and grab the suspect's left arm. Keep the suspect's right handcuffed arm in place, and bring his left arm across to the handcuff.

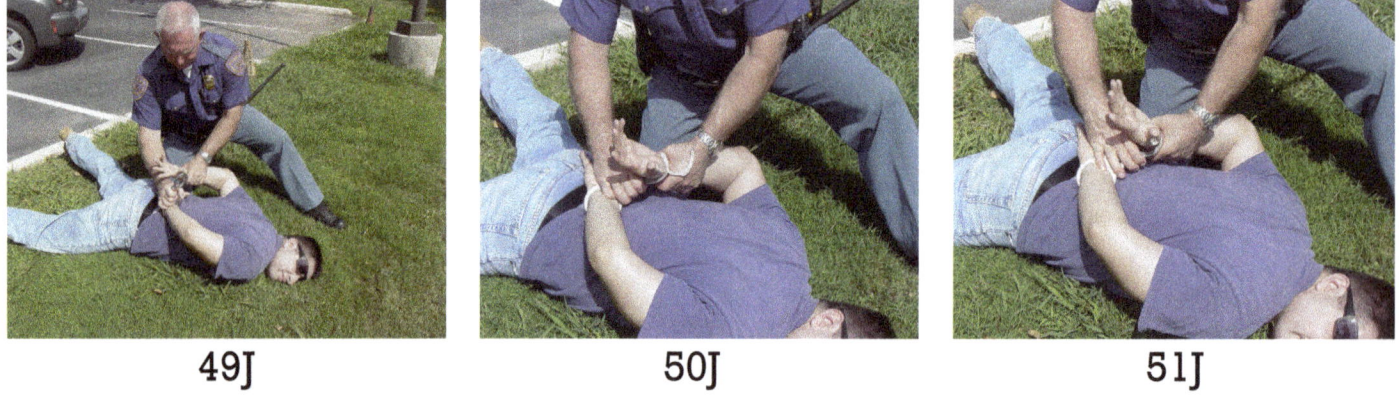

49J  50J  51J

Figures **49J, 50J, and 51J**. Press the suspect's left wrist into the cuff, and make sure it is locked before releasing your right hand from the center of handcuffs.

# Standing Handcuffed Prisoner Technique 2

*This technique is a little different than technique 1, on pages 43-44. Technique 2 works well if the person that you are standing is heavy and needs more assistance. To prevent you from lifting, turn your prisoner onto his knee first.*

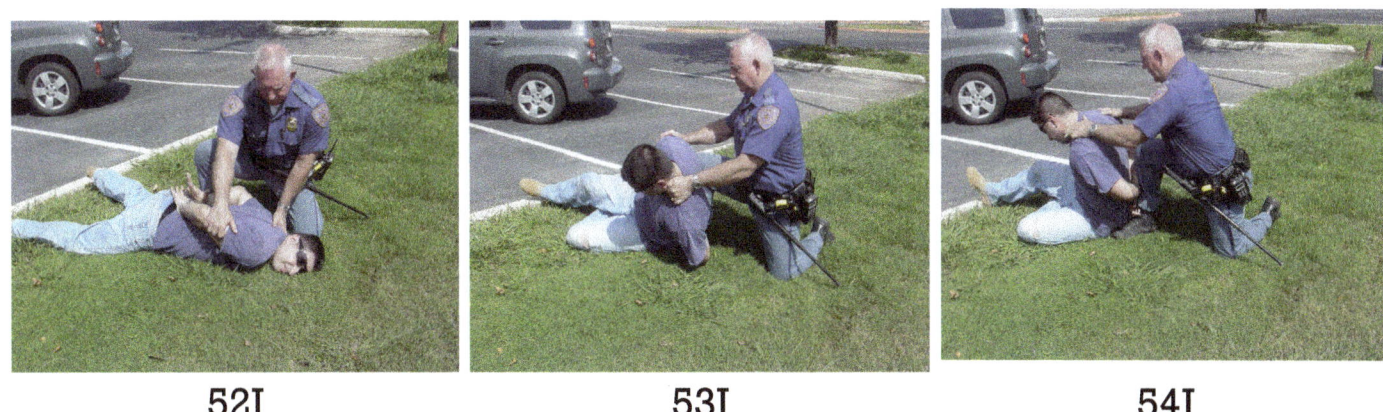

52J  53J  54J

Figures 52J, 53J, and 54J. To turn the suspect over so he is sitting, grab his right shoulder with your right hand. Change your kneeling position to the left knee for better balance. Place your left hand between the shoulder and neck on his left side. Explain to the suspect that your are going to sit him up, as you pull and turn him to sit.

55J  56J  57J

Figures 55J, 56J, and 57J. After he is seated tell him that he should bend his left knee, and that you are going to push him forward onto that knee so he can stand up. Again brace yourself so you will be able to push the suspect over onto his left knee. Place your left hand on his left arm so you will be able to lift, and your right hand on the suspect's back so you can push forward. When he gets to his knees and balanced, you stand up. He may need a little more assistance to stand.

58J  59J  60J

Figure 58J. Before standing the suspect up, place the suspect in a finger lock. Reach inside the handcuffs between the suspect's back and the suspect, and grip his little finger and ring finger, close to his hand.

Figures 59J, and 60J. Make sure your grip is secure on your finger lock, as you explain to the suspect that you are now going to stand him up on his feet. The suspect may need some help. By using your finger lock with your right hand and your left hand on the suspect's right upper arm, push him slightly forward and lift slightly. The suspect will stand, but you will still have control with the finger lock, so he can not run or pull away.

61J  62J

Figures 61J, and 62J. Once the suspect is standing on his feet and has caught his balance, the finger lock is not removed. The control of the finger lock will give you all the control needed to move the suspect from this location to wherever he needs to be taken.

# Chapter 5
# Bent Arm L-Wrist

# Vehicle Extraction Exit V

# Bent Arm L-Wrist

This extraction is the most difficult, but allows you great control over suspects that are unwilling to exit the vehicle. This extraction is not **just** used for unwilling participants, but it is a powerful extraction that when applied, is deceiving to the amount of pressure that appears to be used.

The pictures in the following scenario will show a subject in his vehicle that has already removed his seat belt, but has become uncooperative and unwilling to exit the vehicle. You see the subject gripping the steering wheel tightly and refusing to exit.

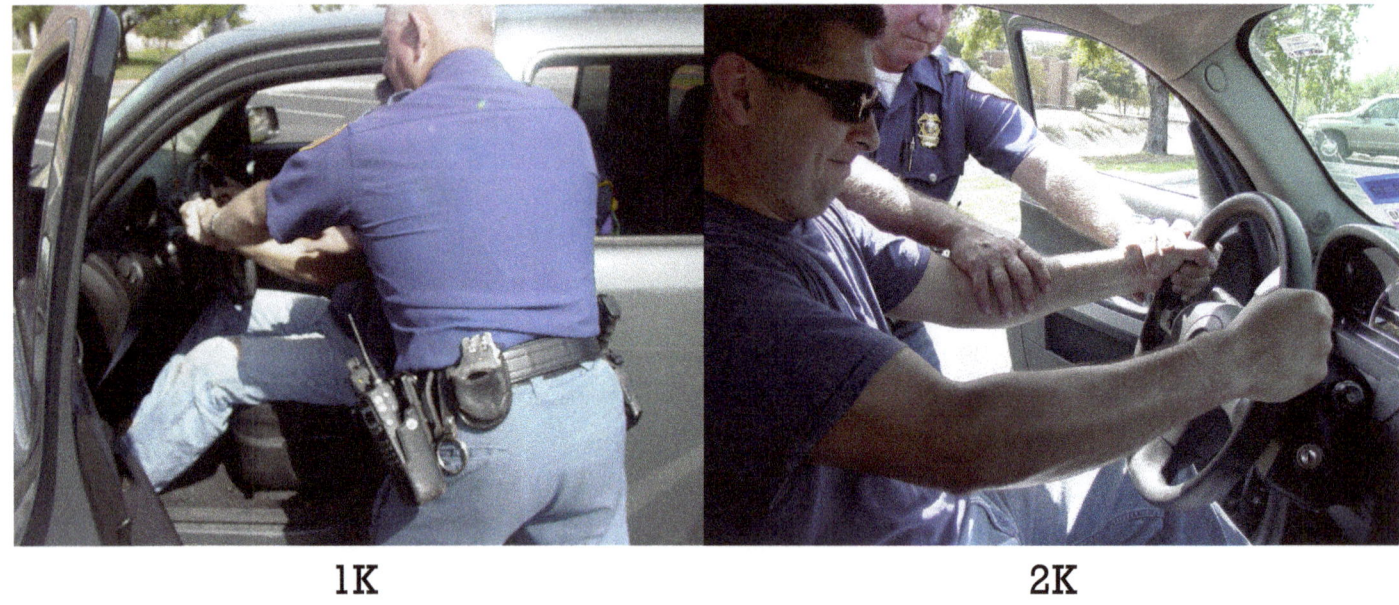

1K                                    2K

Figures 1K, and 2K. After your approach to the suspect's vehicle, you have opened the door and have had the suspect remove his seat belt. Now, he is not cooperating. First, grip the left arm of the suspect with both hands - **one at the wrist and the other at the forearm.** The grip on the suspect's arm plays a major role in releasing the steering wheel with his right hand. This prevents the suspect from trying to backhand you in the face as you approach, if he should decide to let go and fight. The major goal in grabbing the arm is to allow the suspect to develop a **focal point**. The idea is to make the suspect believe that you are going to try to pull his hand from the steering wheel. This will make him focus on his grip on the steering wheel and expect a physical confrontation of strength against strength. He will be expecting the officer to try and pull his hands free from the steering wheel.

3K             4K             5K

Figure 3K. Position yourself with both hands on the suspect's forearm. Pull on the suspect's wrist with your left hand. This will give the appearance of you trying to pull the suspect's left hand off the steering wheel. Allow your right hand to come inside the suspect's left forearm.

Figure 4K. While the suspect is focusing on you pulling his hand off the steering wheel, bend your elbow, pushing it forward into the suspect's left jaw area. This is your distract. Keep your left hand on the suspect's left wrist.

Figure 5K. Reach in front of the suspect's body, keeping your elbow at his jaw line. The left hand is still pulling on the suspect's left wrist, still giving him the illusion that his hand is to be pulled off the steering wheel.

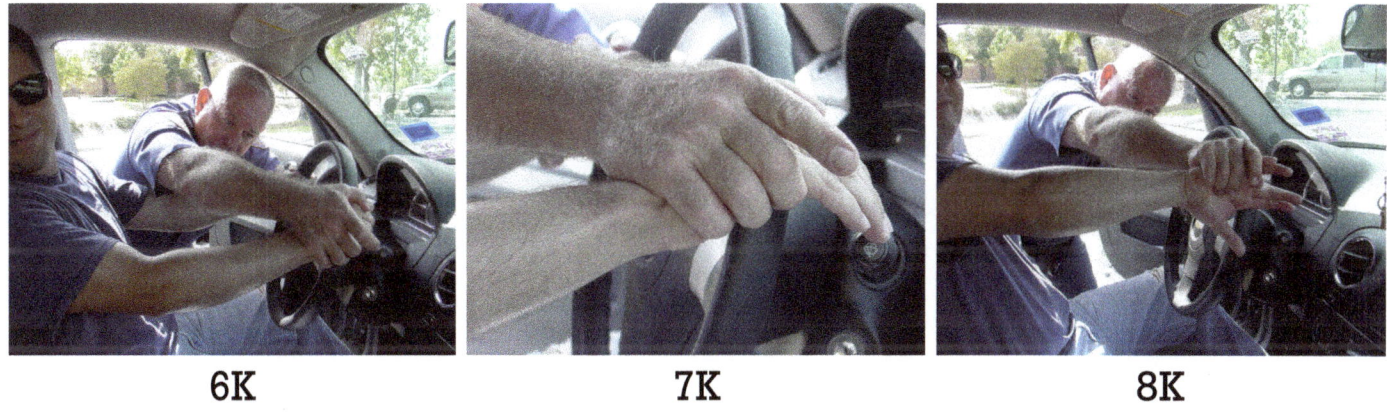

6K             7K             8K

Figure 6K. After the distract, reach quickly to the back of the suspect's right hand. Grab his hand, so your fingers are grabbing the heel portion of the his hand. Peel his hand back toward you, pulling it off the steering wheel.

Figure 7K. Notice the grip on the suspect's right hand. Your fingers should grip the heel of the suspect's hand, and your thumb is back behind the suspect's fingers. Pull back, rolling the suspect's wrist back toward you.

Figure 8K. When the suspect's hand comes free from the steering wheel, it will be turned back toward you. Push your thumb between his fingers for a solid grip.

9K           10K           11K

Figure 9K. When your thumb is pushed between the suspect's fingers, make it a grip that is a strong, comfortable grip for you. This means grabbing the number of fingers in which your grip will be the most powerful. If you have small hands, two fingers will be adequate. If your hands are large, three or four fingers may be comfortable for you. Remember that it is not just your hand size that may make the difference. The suspect's hands will differ in size also.

Figure 10K. Once the suspect's hand is off the steering wheel and your grip is tight, bend his wrist forward, toward his forearm, by bringing his arm closer to his body as you pull his arm out.

Figure 11K. When the wrist is near the front of the suspect's chest, turn your grip upward, which will lock his wrist back toward the roof of the vehicle. Your left hand is still gripping the suspect's left wrist.

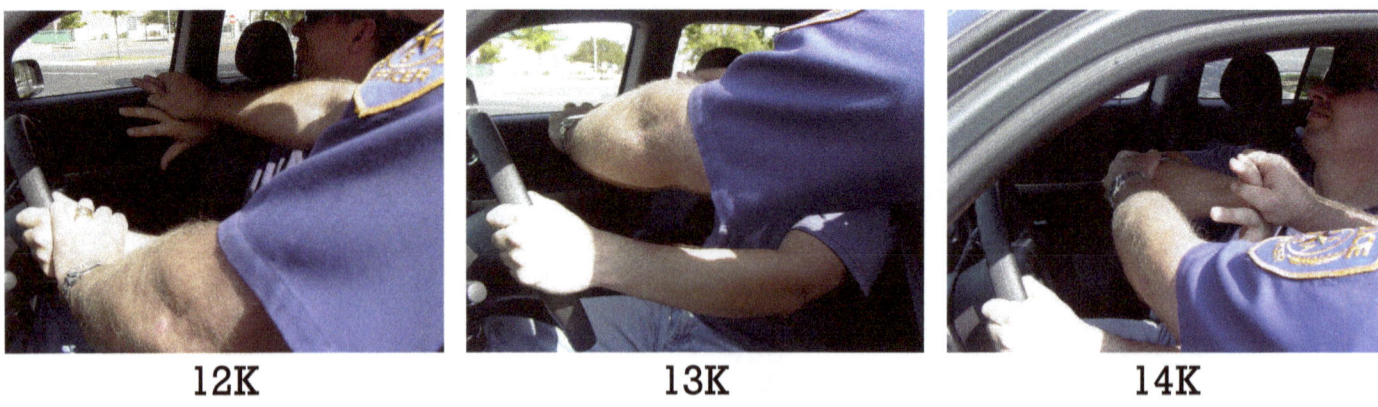

12K           13K           14K

Figure 12K. When pulling the suspect's hand toward you, the wrist bends easily into the correct position when you keep the suspect's hand close to his body, as it is brought across the chest area. Turn your grip upward when it reaches about mid-body on the suspect.

Figures 13K, and 14K. When you turn the grip upward, release your left hand from his wrist. Reach across to assist the suspect's elbow in coming straight across.

15K          16K          17K

Figure 15K. When the suspect's left wrist is released by your left hand, reach in and place your left hand behind the suspect's elbow. Your right hand is still used to keep the suspect's right hand locked.

Figure 16K, and 17K. Assist the suspect's right arm across his body, parallel to the ground. Bring his arm to the open doorway which will cause the suspect to turn his body to his left facing the officer. Apply pressure with the left and right hand, squeezing the suspect's arm in between. **Squeezing** the suspect's arm will assure that your lock will remain tight as he enters the doorway of his vehicle. **NOTE**: The squeeze of the suspect's arm at the doorway is not a tight squeeze but just enough to keep his wrist locked in a forward position.

18K          19K          20K

Figure 18K. Keep the suspect's forearm parallel to the ground while he is still in the vehicle. The wrist is locked in two positions - **locked bent forward and locked bent upward**. It will remain locked as the elbow is brought forward.

Figure 19K. When the suspect's arm has been brought to the opening of the doorway, keep the elbow pulled forward, so he will not be able to pull it back into the car.

Figure 20K. When the suspect's arm is at the threshold of the door, you will see that his body will have to start turning toward you, due to the pressure on his wrist and arm. At this point, you will need to face the vehicle, and bring his arm forward which will keep the tension on his arm and keep him forward and off balance.

 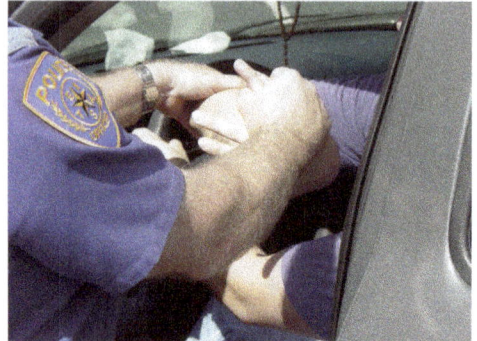 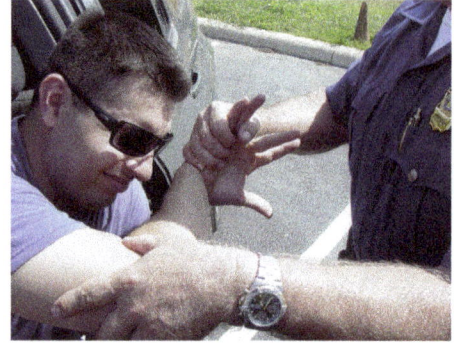

**21K**       **22K**       **23K**

Figures 21K, and 22K. When the suspect has turned toward you at the doorway and pressure is still being placed on the suspect's arm, the suspect's arm needs to be brought forward and made parallel with your chest.

Figure 23K. Keep the suspect's arm parallel with your chest and the ground, and bring the suspect out of the vehicle, leading him with his right arm.

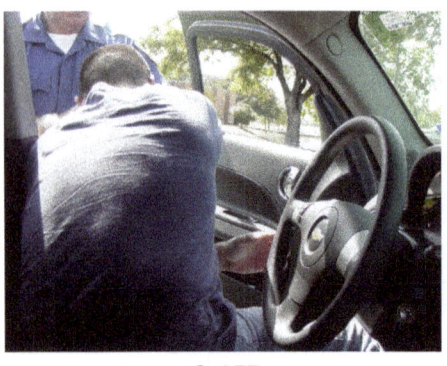  

**24K**       **25K**       **26K**

Figures 24K, 25K, and 26K. When leading the suspect out of the vehicle, take your time. Keep the suspect in the correct position with the wrist locked forward, as well as locked in the turned up position. Your left hand is pulling the suspect's elbow forward to lead him out of the vehicle, as well as keeping the suspect's arm parallel with your chest.

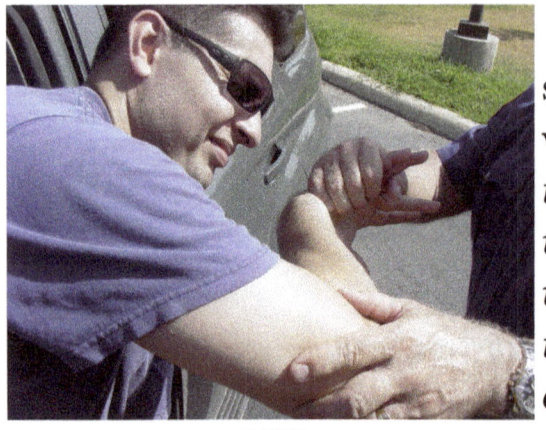

**27K**

Figure 27K. This is a closer look at the correct position of the suspect's arm when coming out of the vehicle. **NOTICE:** *The suspects arm is parallel to the officer's chest. The suspect is being led out of his vehicle arm first. The pressure is still on the locked wrist in both the forward and the turned up position, by the officer's right hand. The left hand of the officer compresses the elbow toward the wrist, while moving the suspect out of the vehicle.*

 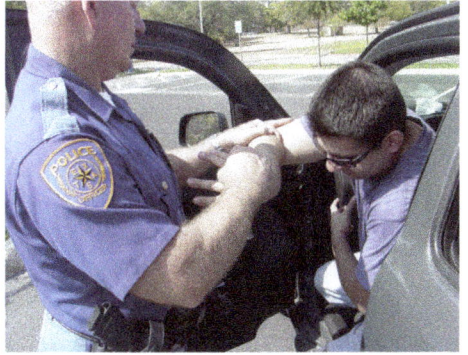 

28K            29K            30K

Figure 28K. Allow the suspect to start exiting the vehicle, watching to make sure that his left foot is flat on the ground when it exits. The officer is squared off with the suspect, and when bringing the suspect out at this point, the suspect's arm is brought out toward the officer, keeping the arm square and parallel with the chest.

Figure 29K. Keeping the suspect's arm in your grip may mean having to adjust the arm, as the suspect exits the vehicle. The adjustments may be a small amount, but it needs to be kept up with. **HELPFUL HINT** and for better control on the suspect's elbow with your left hand - keep three fingers to the rear of the suspect's elbow, and place the index finger at the bent side of the elbow. This will continue the pressure between the suspect's wrist and elbow, and the use of the index finger will keep the suspect's arm parallel to the chest of the officer.

Figure 30K. When the suspect's body reaches the halfway point out of the doorway, the officer prepares to take a step back with his right foot.

  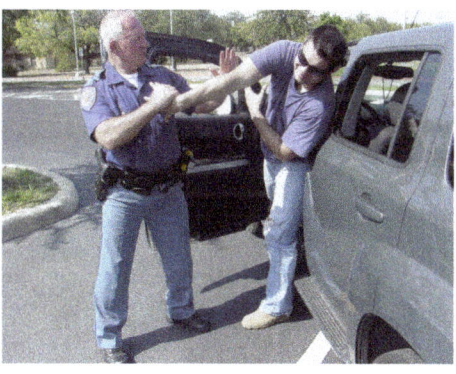

31K            32K            33K

Figures 31K, and 32K. The officer has stepped back with his right foot, giving room and direction for the suspect to exit. The suspect will be moved to the right of the officer and alongside the suspect's vehicle.

Figure 33K. The officer will straighten the suspect's arm by pulling the suspect's right hand, and then pushing forward with the left hand behind the elbow. This is the start of the takedown from the bent arm L-wrist extraction.

# Extraction Takedown From Bent Arm L-Wrist

The takedown for the bent arm L-wrist is unlike the other takedowns in this extraction program. The main difference is that the area being stressed is not the elbow, like the other extractions, now the control is on the hand and wrist of the suspect. The control of the suspect's hand and wrist are controlled by the grip that the officer has on the hand. **NOTE:** *The officer is able to continue a control over the suspect while the suspect's arm is still bent. The control of the bent arm can be used to move the suspect prior to the takedown.*

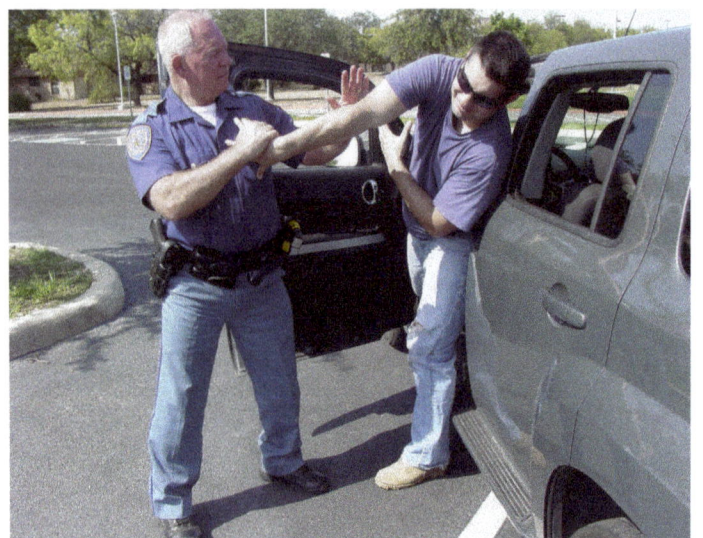

1L

2L

Figure 1L. You are ready to take the suspect down to the ground after you hyperextend the suspect's right arm. The officer's right foot has now stepped back, giving the necessary room for the suspect to pass in front of the officer. Place your left hand behind the suspect's elbow, creating a fulcrum. **NOTE**: *When putting pressure on the suspect's elbow, <u>do not</u> strike the back of the elbow with your left hand when straightening it. This may cause injury to the suspect's elbow.*

Figure 2L. While placing pressure behind the suspect's elbow with your left hand, allow your right hand to come down even with the suspect's hips, as the suspect's right shoulder rolls forward. If you keep the suspect's right hand high, as soon as his shoulder starts to roll forward, he may roll forward causing you to lose the grip and control. The suspect's arm still needs to be perpendicular to his body.

 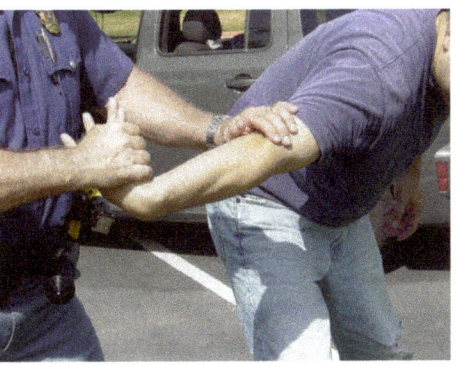 

3L　　　　　　　　　4L　　　　　　　　　5L

Figures 3L, and 4L. When the officer applies the pressure to the suspect's arm, he needs to be beside the suspect. Notice that the fingers of the officer's left hand are forward and around toward the front of the suspect's arm. This is one more precaution that is taken if the suspect tries to roll forward when going to the ground. This will allow the officer to pull back with his left hand, bending the suspect's elbow and again place him in the bent arm elbow position.

Figure 5L. The officer steps forward with his right foot for balance, as the suspect goes to his hand and knees onto the ground. The right arm of the suspect is still out to his side, even with his body.

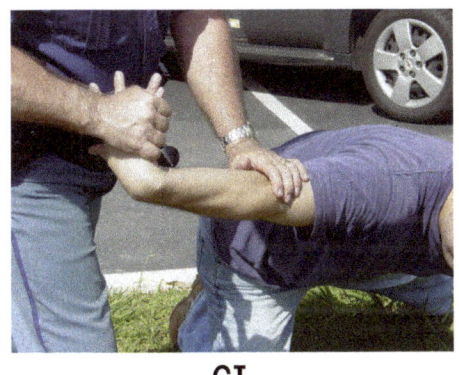 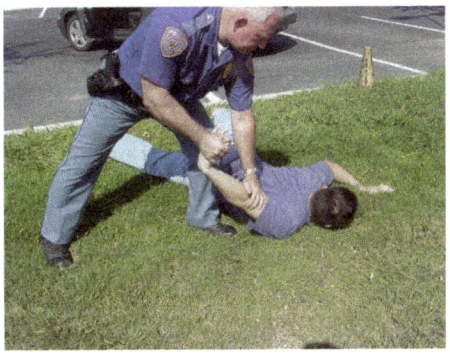 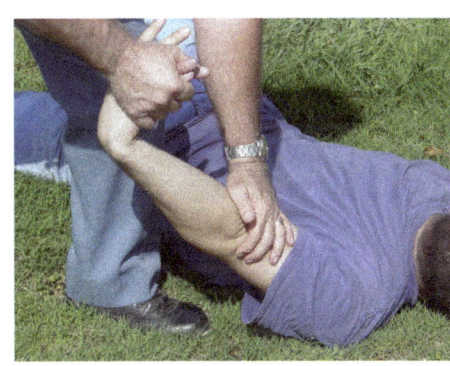

6L　　　　　　　　　7L　　　　　　　　　8L

Figure 6L. While the suspect is on his knees, his arm is extended to the side, even with his body, and the hand is locked inward, as well as locked forward.

Figures 7L, and 8L. When the suspect lies on the ground, the right hand is now higher than the suspect's body. This will allow pressure to be placed down on the suspect's shoulder with the officer's right hand, as the left hand keeps the suspect's elbow straight. Pressing the shoulder to the ground will stop the suspect from turning to the side. The officer stands close to the suspect with his left foot and slightly leaned forward, so pressure is directed down the arm to the suspect's shoulder.

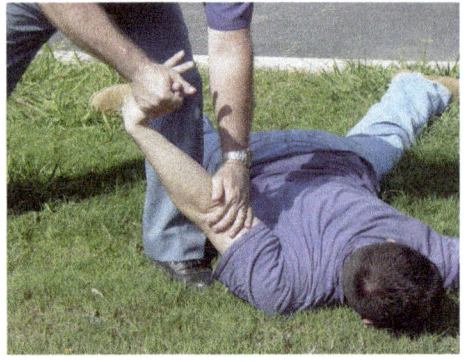  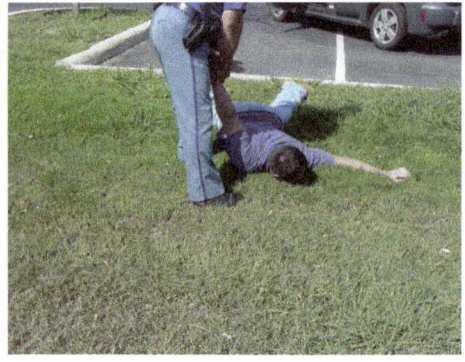

9L            10L            11L

Figure 9L. Make sure that the suspect's arm is locked and straight and that the shoulder is firmly pressed against the ground.

Figures 10L, and 11L. Release the left hand from the suspect's elbow, and stand upright. Step forward with your right foot so that you are facing the suspect's right side, and stand over his right arm. Pull up on the suspect's right wrist, keeping the arm straight.

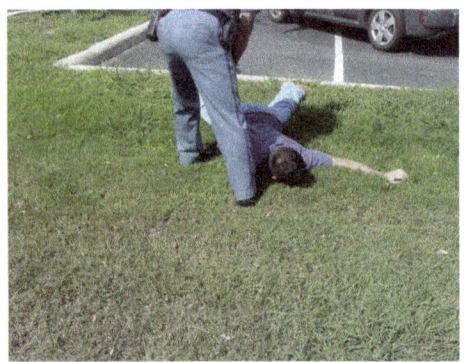 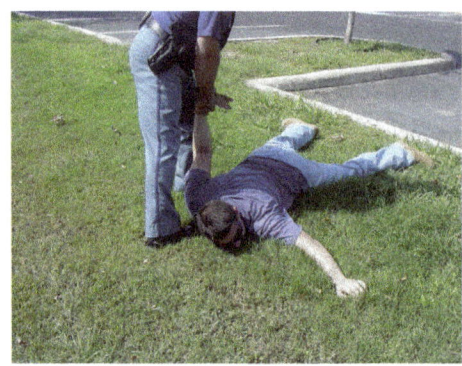 

12L            13L            14L

Figures 12L, 13L, and 14L. Step to the top of the suspect's right shoulder with your right foot, sliding your toes under the right shoulder. The Figures shown have this broken down so you can see what angle to bring your foot in under the shoulder. This is just one easy step, bringing your foot around and sliding it under the suspect's

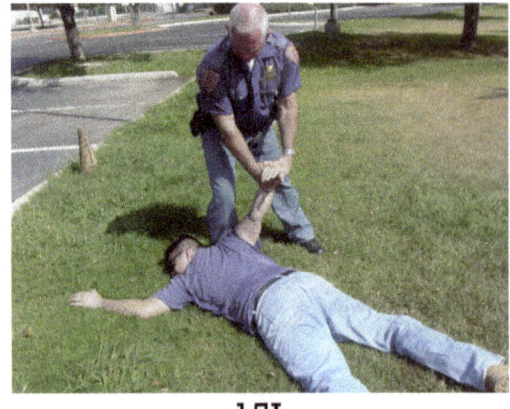

Figures 15L and 16L. Keep pulling upward on the suspect's wrist, as you now make a large step with your left leg from the suspect's right side back behind you.

15L

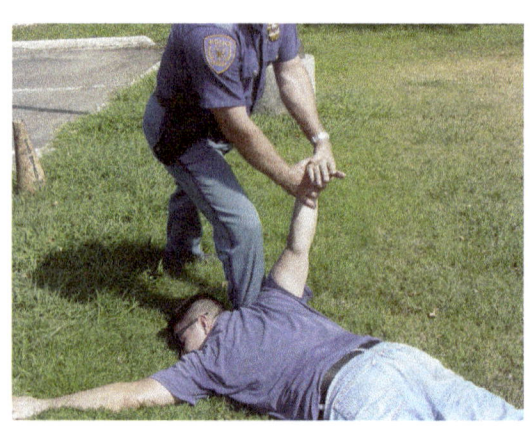

16L

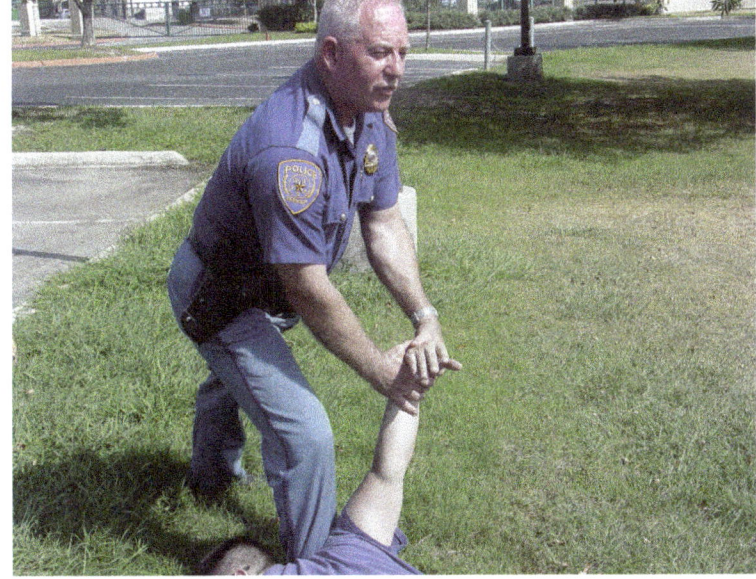

Figure 17L. This position is very important. First, after your left foot steps back, the suspect's arm is pulled back toward you. This will lock the shoulder and arm of the suspect. Secondly, this is where you need to **slow yourself down** and **take a deep breath**, and **observe** what is going on around you. You are able to keep control of the suspect and take your eyes off him to look around to see if anyone else may be involved, and

17L

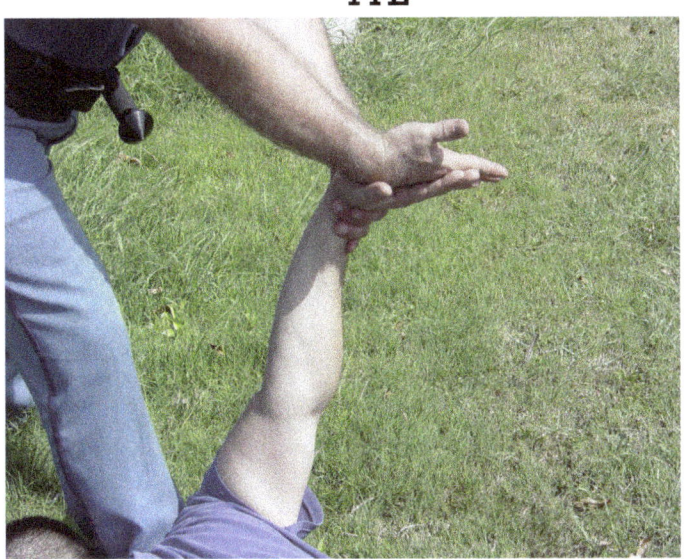

18L

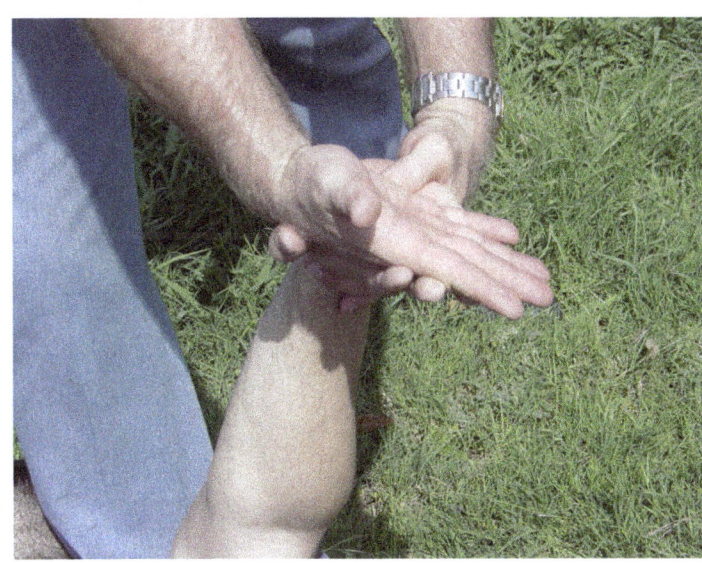

19L

Figures 18L, and 19L. Have the suspect's fingers point toward his feet. Keep the suspect's wrist bent back, and position your left hand right under the bend of the wrist. I use the back of my right hand to open the suspect's hand and to keep the wrist bent back and flat.

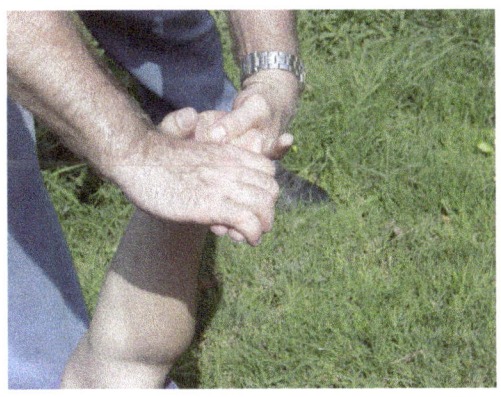

20L

Figures 20L, and 21L. Turn your right hand over so you are palm to palm. Grab deep into the hand and grab two or three fingers. Allow the thumb of your left hand to assist in keeping the wrist bent back and flat.

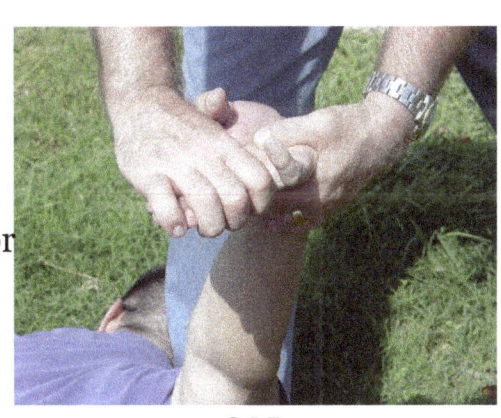

21L

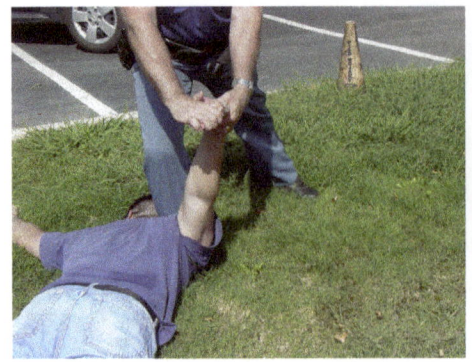 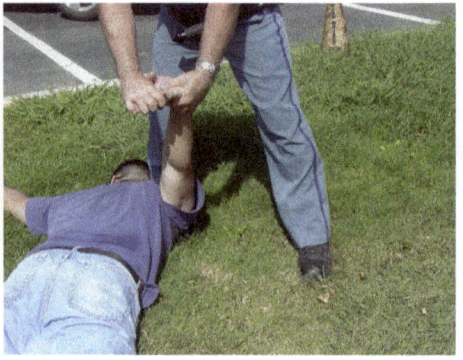 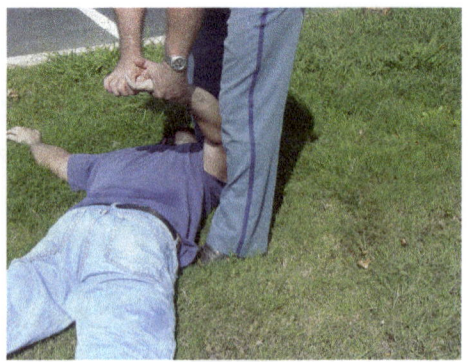

**22L**        **23L**        **24L**

Figure **22L**. When your grip on the suspect's hand is secure and the arm is pulled back against your shin, turn the suspect's hand inward, <u>**SLOWLY**</u> so as not to injure the suspect. When this technique is done correctly, there is an automatic response to the locking of the wrist and fingers at the same time. When the tension hits a lock out position, the suspect's heels will raise or a knee will attempt to come to the side.

Figures **23L, and 24L**. After you have gotten a response to the turning of the suspect's hand, the arm is taken down to the back of the suspect. At the same time, your right foot takes a large step from behind you all the way to the suspect's waistline. The step is one smooth step.

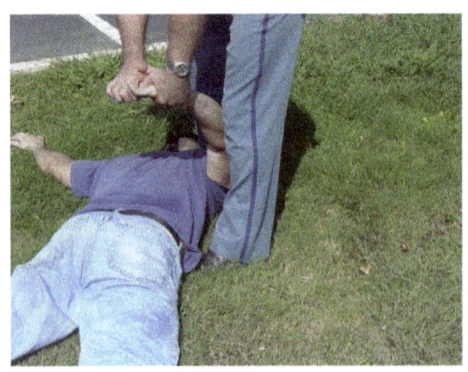 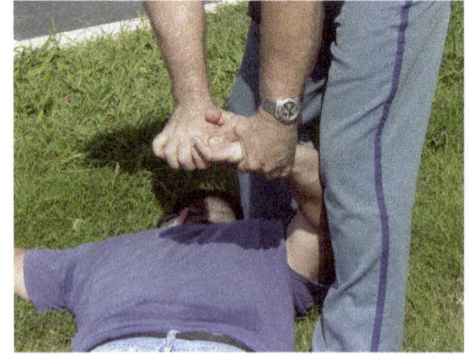 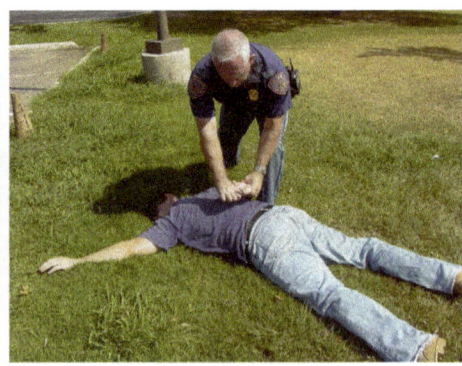

**25L**        **26L**        **27L**

Figures **25L, and 26L**. Taking the arm down to the suspect's back needs to be done slowly and not forced. A great amount of tension is being placed on the suspect's arm in many different areas: fingers, wrist, shoulder, and elbow. So take your time. Use your left hand to flatten out the wrist as it comes down to the suspect's back. The grip of your left hand now slips up on the suspect's wrist, and the thumb stays in the suspect's palm, as the arm comes down to his back.

Figure **27L**. When the suspect's hand gets to his back, your right leg will take a large step back, as you also start to come down alongside of the suspect to kneel.

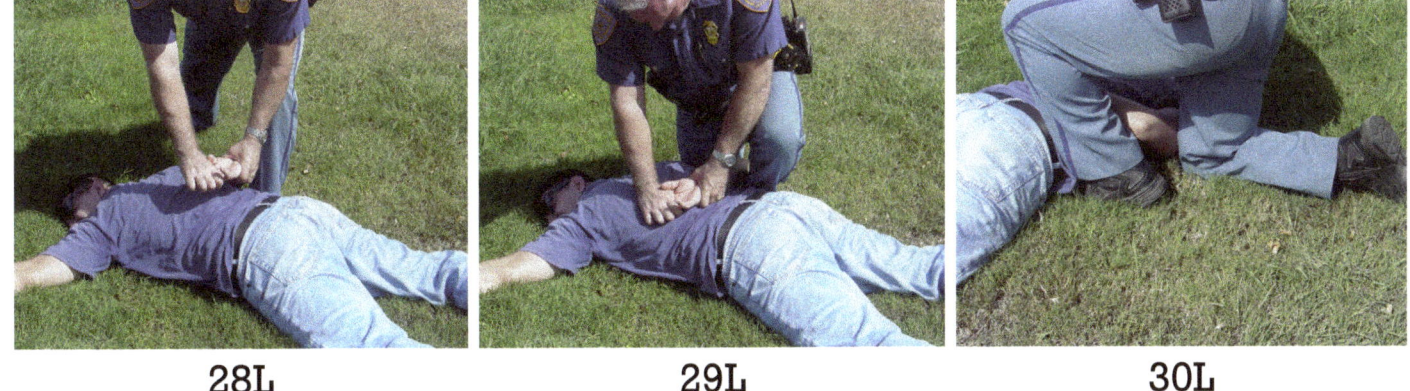

28L           29L           30L

Figure 28L. After the suspect's arm is placed across his back, you can see that the officer's left leg is in a position that will not allow the suspect to push his arm down toward his feet. The right leg of the officer is back way behind.

Figure 29L. When the right leg of the officer is brought forward, the knee will strike the back of the suspect's upper arm, assisting you in pushing the hand across the back, giving you the extra room you will need to handcuff.

Figure 30L. This angle will show how both legs of the officer are used to prevent any movement from the suspect's arm, allowing your hand to reach your handcuffs.

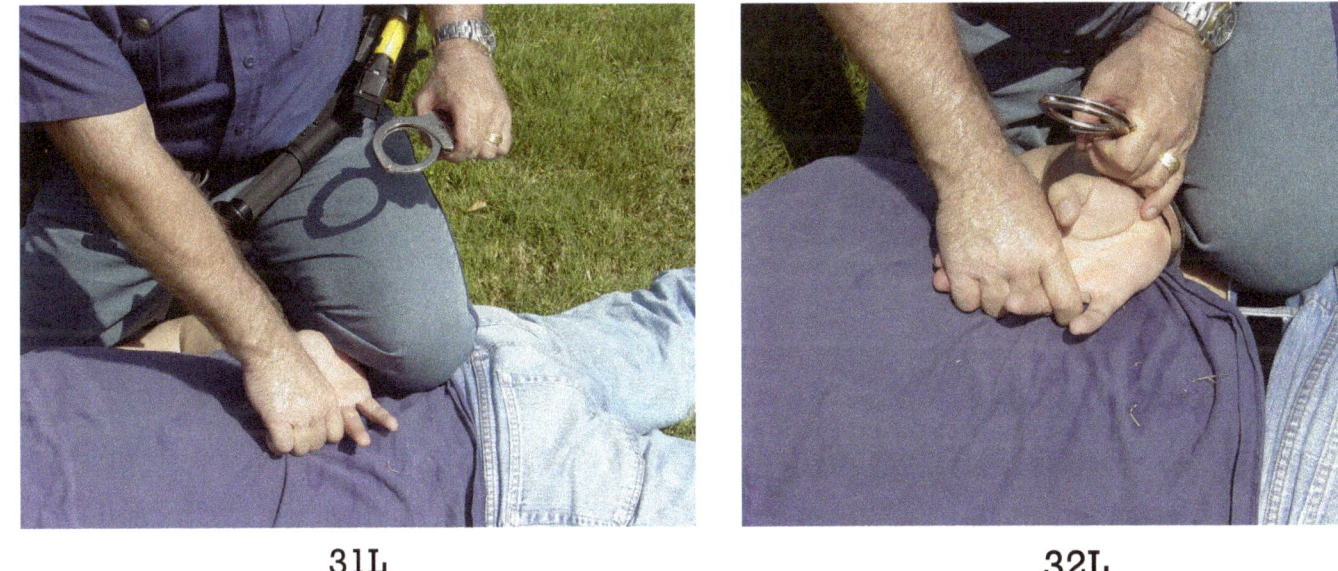

31L           32L

Figure 31L. The officer has lowered his knee across the small of the suspect's back and in front of the suspect's arm. To maintain control, the officer has placed the suspect in a finger lock. The finger lock will allow the officer to raise the suspect's wrist off his back to have room to place the handcuffs on the suspect.

Figure 32L. Raise the wrist, and place the handcuffs on the suspect's wrist. Make sure that there is plenty of room for the cuff to close and that they are locked and not too loose.

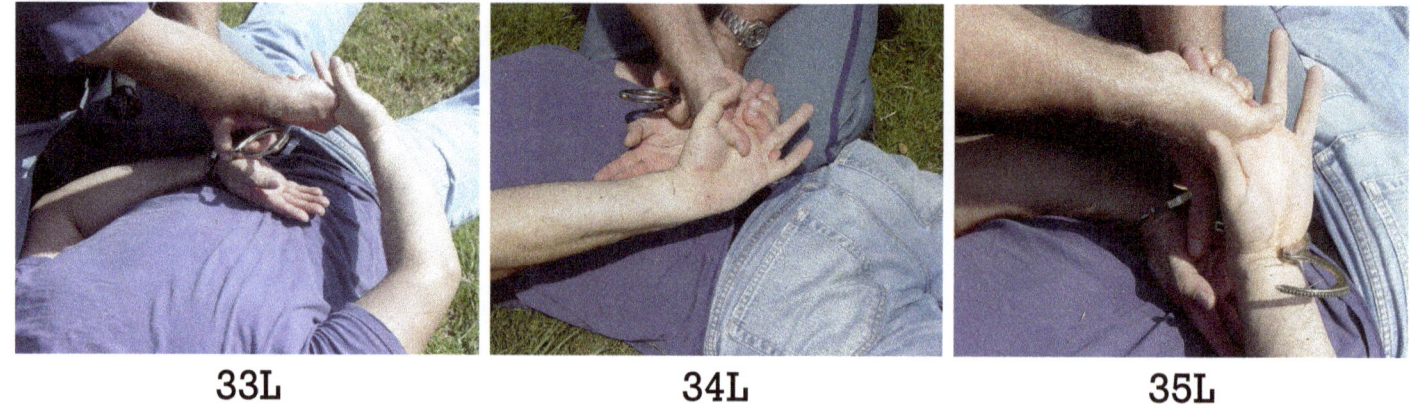

33L  34L  35L

Figure 33L, and 34L. The handcuffed hand will be held by the left hand, as the officer tells the suspect to give him the other hand. When the suspect reaches back with his left hand, the officer grips the hand in a finger lock and pulls it across the back. The suspect's hand is pulled across and in front of the cuffed hand.

Figure 34L. The suspect's left hand is brought in front of the cuffed hand and placed in the handcuff. The cuffed hand will still be supported by the officer holding the handcuff, as the other hand is pushed against the cuff to allow it to open.

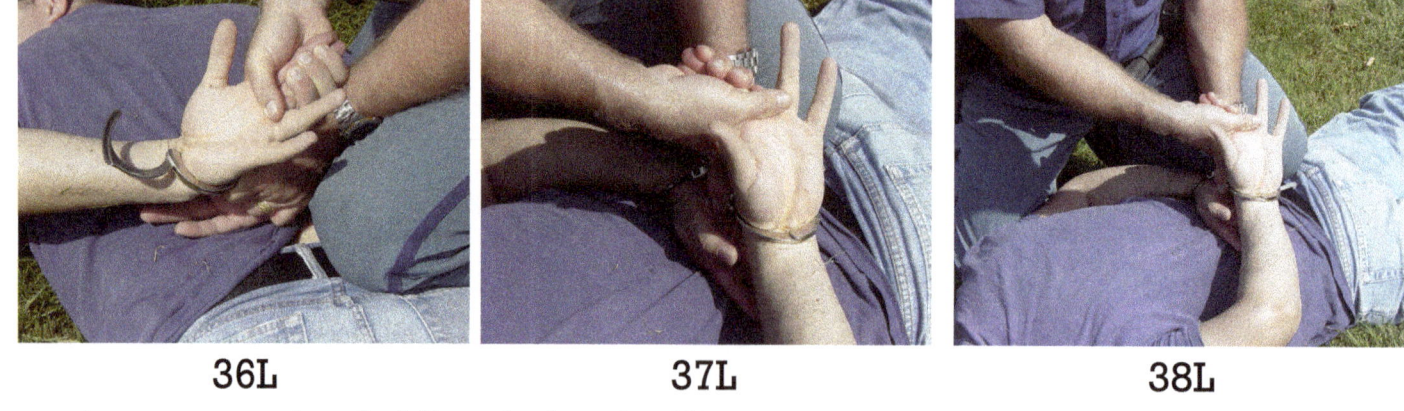

36L  37L  38L

Figure 36L. When holding the handcuff in your left hand, try to take the unused portion of the cuff to the top. This will allow you to bring the suspect's hand across the top of the cuffed hand, and press it against the cuff to open it.

Figures 37L, and 38L. When the left hand of the suspect is placed into the cuff, make sure the cuff locks. Physically and visually check the cuff before releasing the hands.

# CLOSING

It has been a real pleasure to do this book and work with the many individuals that have made this possible. I want to thank the many officers that have purchased this book, and all the books related to the safety of police officers everywhere. If only one of these techniques can save an officer's life or even prevent him from being injured, I have done my job.

The challenges of our job and what we do on the streets is constantly changing and as we evolve, I look forward to updating techniques that will help in the safety and the well- being of officers working in the field. These classes and books are for all officers out there that are interested in increasing their arsenal of techniques to better themselves. By continuing your education and increasing your skills as a police officer, the security of you, your fellow officers and the community you patrol can become a safer place.

Take care of your brother officer, be safe, and God Speed.

Sincere thanks,

*Gary G. Albrecht*

www.ingramcontent.com/pod-product-compliance
Lightning Source LLC
Chambersburg PA
CBHW061117170426
43199CB00026B/2954